MY FATHER ON EARTH AS HE IS IN HEAVEN

Peg Snyder

ISBN 979-8-89112-394-6 (Paperback)
ISBN 979-8-89112-395-3 (Digital)

Scripture taken from the HOLY BIBLE, NEW INTERNATIONAL VERSION copyright © 1973, 1978, 1984 International Bible Society. Used by permission of Zondervan Bible Publishers

Covenant Books
11661 Hwy 707
Murrells Inlet, SC 29576
www.covenantbooks.com

In honor of William (Bill) Schuhler, who gave his
life for his wife and children and imparted more
than I could have ever known into my life.
And my heavenly Father God, who so graciously and
lovingly has continued to unfold Himself to me throughout
my entire life, even before I acknowledged Him.

I will sing of the Lord's great love forever;
with my mouth I will make your faithfulness
known through all generations.

I will declare that your love stands firm
forever, that you established your faithfulness in
heaven itself. (Psalm 89:1–2 NIV)

CONTENTS

My deepest gratitude to Jay, my husband, the faithful love of my life for more than forty years. You have unceasingly encouraged me, stood by me, and exemplified the Father's love to me and our family. You didn't allow me to give up on the dream of putting these words into print.

PREFACE

What an incredible year. It had challenged me beyond anything I'd experienced as of yet in my forty-eight years. I am here to tell of a victory, though, unequal to any other—a victory of faith, a victory of love.

Jesus, on February 1, 2006, when I had the vision of You taking my hand quietly, gently at the edge of the desert and proceeding forward into the vast expanse of barrenness, nothingness as far as our eyes could see, well, I had no idea. My thoughts were of heading into a thirty-day fast together—that it would be a difficult journey much like other desert places in life. You were leading, though, so it would be okay. And I felt peace. I voiced my trust in You. I recommitted myself to a deeper level of Your Lordship over my life. I felt safe with You there, and I knew Your constant unspoken assurance that You would never leave me. I would do my best to be as faithful to You. A thirty-day fast—a new challenge that I wasn't sure I was up to, but at least now I knew that it *was* Your will for me, and I would go.

On February 1, 2007, I recalled the vision going into the desert and realized that the entire year of 2006 had been just that, a desert. There was a time when I thought I was coming out—several times actually. They were only mirages, visions of comfort that quickly faded into more pain, more pressing on, further testing and agony. At those times of teasing relief, I saw myself as one "coming up from the desert, leaning on her lover" in a fashion of me resting my head on Your shoulder. The next time it was as though You bore much of my weight as I leaned hard onto You. Another time, I was so hard-pressed onto Your side that we were inseparable. Finally, on January 20, 2007, however, the clearest image appeared as I stood completely exhausted, broken, dried up, pitiful, with the most shriveled-up, dried-out, ugliest leathery heart I'd ever seen. I stood in a pool of uncontrollable tears as You revealed the outcome of the year's trial on my heart. How had this happened? I tried so hard to be faithful, to hold my heart open even when death seemed determined to destroy it. I had not let go of You but held on when it seemed as though there was nothing to grasp. As I stood there, horrified, overwhelmed with the agony of my heart's condition, while my two dear friends flanked each side and my forehead fell forward, resting—no, leaning hard into my husband's forehead, being held up by his firm embrace, the full truth was revealed.

This is how You wanted me all along. It is now I, Your beloved, coming up from the desert, leaning on her lover in a fashion where I face You and see You alone. I no longer have vision for anything else but You. I am fully supported, held up and sustained by my Lover. Without You, I cannot take a single step, for I can't see where I'm going, nor do I have any strength of my own. We are truly inseparable. If I were to try to separate, I would crumble and die. I only feel Your warmth, Your strength, Your breath. There is nothing else. I no longer lean on Your side. We are face-to-face, and You move me forward into Your will, into what You see, into where You desire to go. The movement is like it's effortless on my part. My effort is fully absorbed in keeping myself ever before You—leaning into You, gazing into You.

Did You delight in seeing my heart in this despicable condition? Was this Your desire? No, not for a second. But my position and perspective of being completely melted into You, that was an element of great beauty, much as a jewel glimmering in Your hands.

If you have no ability to envision this, perhaps you can better relate to my experience as a little girl with my dad. Dad loved to celebrate with dancing and funny little jigs. Weddings were a favorite time to dance and celebrate. One of my most treasured childhood memories is of dancing at weddings with my dad. Sometimes he would lift me up into his arms, sandwiched between him and Mom, while they danced. This was generally accompanied by abundant bouncing and laughter. But sometimes, if it was just the two of us, Dad would let my feet ride on top of his and we'd giggle and glide together across the floor effortlessly for me, *with my eyes riveted on his, while he bore all of my weight, fully in control of our movement.* This is the picture of where I have come to rest with my heavenly Father today. I have come full circle to my Daddy who carries me while my eyes are riveted on Him. Well, actually, it's not yet completely full circle with an important component yet to be restored. In those early days, as a little girl, there was present an innocent joy, giggling, fun. As I came up from the desert on January 20, 2007, though the depth of love that strengthened me was overwhelming, and the peace and rest ran deep, I sensed only the planting of joy. I hold the hope of a joy not yet brought to full maturity, waiting to be nourished and watered so it can blossom into full fruition. Then I will have come full circle, fully knowing my Father in heaven as I knew my father on earth. But we are dancing. Won't you come and join us? My Dad has boundless feet. He can carry us all!

I sincerely hope the pages to follow will lead you into a greater discovery of who our heavenly Father is, gliding us across the foundations of life into that place of trusting with full dependence on Him. I hope you will find a place where past pain and disappointments can safely land so they can be traded for peace, hope, and a fresh planting of joy to be nurtured in your life.

INTRODUCTION

This is my journey of discovery. Through these stories, you will find real life experiences, mostly my experiences, that have facilitated my understanding of who God is. They highlight how He is involved in our lives even when we are unaware. It is the framework of a personal relationship with a Creator that, for some reason, chose to call Himself our Father and us His children.

To enhance your understanding of the accounts I write about, I would like to briefly introduce you to my family.

My parents, Alice and Bill, have a legendary love story of being teenage sweethearts who were torn apart by World War II. After just one semester of playing college football (his dream come true), he answered the call to duty along with scores of other young patriotic men, by joining the US Navy. (Side note: This was always funny for us to think about considering my dad never learned to swim his entire life!) Upon my dad's departure (he was twenty and my mom was eighteen), they got engaged and agreed to be married when he returned. Little did they know what was ahead. My dad was caught up in the world gone wild at war and was part of the South Pacific fleet for two years solid without ever seeing his homeland. They communicated faithfully by letter, which came delivered in groups at a time, with huge gaps in between. The first leave he got to come home, he sent word to my mom. She had not much more than a week to put together their wedding, which was performed in full style with friends and relatives donating food coupons (rationing of goods was still in full operation due to the war) so they could have a wedding cake and food for a reception. My mom had sewn her wedding gown in advance and had bridesmaids' gowns, complete with a flower girl in appropriately made lace and ruffles. When my dad arrived, they had just a couple of days to get reacquainted before they said vows, pledging their lifetime commitment to one another. Their bold, courageous love was shocking really! I have always marveled at how after being separated worlds apart for two whole years, they remained faithful and sure of their devotion. Once they were wed, Dad was off again to California. Mom was able to follow him later, and they stayed until the war ended shortly after.

Upon returning back home after the war, they were eager to begin a normal family life. They wasted no time in beginning their plan. My oldest sister arrived about a year and a half after they said "I do." Family life overtook them rapidly, which I believe, after the traumatic experience of the war, they were thankful for.

We ended up being seven children in all, all from the same parents. While this may be an unusual phenomenon today, it was much more "normal" in my childhood years. I will admit, however, that most families of our size were immediately identified as "good Catholics." That was, in fact, true in our case. We were raised to go to church *every* Sunday, *all* of us. If you lived in our house, you went to church. The fear of eternity in the flames caused us to honor that commitment above all others. Even though I no longer practice Catholicism, I still today honor my parents' faithfulness to the church and to God. It taught me many good principles for life in spite of the few stumbling blocks I needed to overcome later in my faith walk. I consider my family's faith a foundation of strength in my upbringing. My own recognition of the need for a personal relationship with Jesus did not come until I was a young adult on my own, through a Bible study. In spite of my faithful Catholicism, I had missed the part about salvation by grace through faith in Jesus until I read it myself in Ephesians 2:8–9, "For it is by grace you have been saved, through faith—and this not from yourselves, it is the gift of God—not by works, so that no one can boast."

The children in my family comprised of six girls and one boy. I know. I heard it all my life. "Your poor brother!" My response to that was always the same. No, sir, he's not poor! He's the only one to have his own room and his own clothes not of hand-me-downs or shared. My lone brother was quite beloved by us all. His personality was not one of an aggressive antagonist but one of a gentle, yet strong, somewhat comical prankster who was full of life. He was the second born and faced much disappointment in his young life as time after time, his hopes of a brother were crushed with the arrival of baby sister after baby sister. As the sixth child (the fifth daughter), I was told that when I was born, my brother shed great volumes of crocodile tears with a crushed heart. Apparently, by the time my younger sister, the last born, came to be, however, there was no such drama because my brother had abandoned his hopes. Instead, he embraced me and my younger sister with such exuberant, fun-loving affection that we absolutely adored him!

Our family was also somewhat divided into "the older ones" and "the younger ones." The later was comprised of the three youngest girls and were considered "spoiled" by the older ones. Knowing what I do now, I am quite certain the older four had a quite different experience with our parents than I did. I am thankful to be on the later end to be honest. Our parents gained much wisdom with each child.

The older ones comprised of the first three children being approximately thirteen months apart and no. 4 just a couple of years later. My poor parents had four children, five and under at one time. The rest of us were a little more spread out. There were fourteen and a half years between the oldest and the youngest. It was a challenge for even the bravest, best parenting skills, I'm sure.

Personality-wise, my mom was quite a strong-willed, ambitious woman. She raised every one of her daughters to be strong as well, although we all expressed it differently. At one point, amid my own parenting challenges with our three young children, I told my mom that I felt I had three kids who were all polar opposites from one another. In a "misery loves company" sort of way, my mom tried to encourage me by saying that all seven of us in our family were opposites! We girls were as different as could be. The oldest was responsible, more of an athlete, and had more of my dad's easygoing personality. The third was fiery and full of personality that demanded to be heard one way or another. The fourth was quiet with an inner strength and will that found its way regardless of whatever else was happening. The fifth was an exuberant, ambitious athlete that embraced the role of leading the younger pack. Then me, the sixth, full of energy that sometimes stirred the pot a bit too much amongst the younger crowd with a prominent stubborn streak. And lastly, the seventh, the always-curious social butterfly of the group, loved by all with that strong will so well hidden beneath her sweetness that it was easy for others to give into what she wanted.

Growing up, we shared bedrooms, beds, clothes, bathrooms, baths, toys, bikes, chores, food, and responsibility for screwups when no one would fess up. We were taught to work things out between us. I am convinced that living in close quarters with so many different personalities plays a huge part in why I am able to relate so easily to such a varied number of people in different social settings both within the United States and out of the country.

My parents' devotion rubbed off on us. They were devoted to their faith, family, each other, and their country. It was evident through every stage of their lives together. They modeled to us an ever-growing, ever-changing lifestyle that encouraged us all to embrace the opportunities before us. It was a solid foundation for the premise of this chapter in life where we had been scattered through-out the country in our careers and family choices. Two of us lived in Minnesota, one lived in Florida not far from our parents, and four still lived in Indiana where we were raised. Considering the miles between us, we remained surprisingly close. It was evident during that challenging season when my dad was suffering the severe effects of a stroke he was not expected to survive. In fact, it was said that if he did survive, he'd be a complete invalid. God worked miraculously, though, and gave us seven blessed months with him following that devastating event.

My story is an attempt to help those who lack a positive role model of "father" and, therefore, struggle with such an imagery for God. May a layer of the veil that clouds your vision and understand-ing be lifted to enable you to see our heavenly Father's true character more clearly. I want to bring enlightenment into what a father can be, especially in the divine sense of the role, as heavenly Father. In the years it has taken me to unravel these concepts, God has continued to reveal Himself with increasing insight. It has come piece by piece, bit by bit. As His children, we are meant to be continually growing, maturing, gaining wisdom and strength. You can't hardly stop a child's physical growth unless there's serious malnutrition and depravation. A normal child just automatically grows. God meant for our lives to mimic that of a child's in the aspect of experiencing constant growth under His care. The potential for growth is present all the way until we breathe our last breath on earth.

It is my hope that this will be a venue of nourishment that is provided in your life for your spiritual and relational growth with our good Father in heaven.

1

Never Too Old to Learn

If there's one thing I have learned in my life, it's that I never need to stop learning. There's always more, something beyond my current understanding and knowledge. This goes for the physical world as well as the spiritual. With continuous growth in mind, life always holds something within to reveal a new aspect of our heavenly Father's character. I was amazed that in the last seven months of my natural dad's life here on earth, I felt like I learned more from him than all my adult years combined. He was at his weakest point in life. As he struggled to maintain mental focus and the ability to reason, think, and be logical, something more beautiful emerged from his heart. The depth of love that began to flow from him in the form of humility, appreciation, sincere gratitude, encouragement, compassion, and a hunger for eternity were all wrapped in a cloak of overwhelming sweetness.

I had known Dad as a man of strength. I had long before recognized his ability to discern a person's character, coupled with a gift of wisdom. His love for me was never a question in my heart—not ever—even though it wasn't until his last years that I actually remember hearing those specific words voiced by him. Yet loving words of affirmation and encouragement flowed freely from his heart to accompany me from as far back as I could remember. So what was so new? What had changed? What was so different in those last seven months of his life? A sense of sweetness oozed from him as a thick flowing honey, pouring out, overflowing, sticking to all he came in contact with, blanketing them with a rich, irresistible warmth. It was part of what caused Mom, Dad's wife of sixty-one years, to confess months after his death that those last seven months they had together were the best of their entire marriage.

How could this new richness in Dad be authentic with all his limitations? Rehabilitation efforts after his stroke required large doses of patience, hope, and strength that far exceeded any of our abilities, including the eternal optimist, Mom. Physical limitations left him dependent on constant assistance, with independence always just barely beyond his reach. The torment of being left with a child-like young boyish mind vexed him endlessly and led to regular emotional outbursts inappropriate for a man of such dignity and wisdom. He suffered seemingly uncontrollable tears of anguish, depression, and frustration over limitations that penetrated body and soul alike. Outbursts of anger and impatience threatened to mask the new sweetness that permeated his being, but these were usually followed by moments of childlike repentance. It was heartbreaking and irresistibly sweet.

There was something else too. It was unsettling to some. I found it fascinating. Beautiful. Enticing. Curious. In his brokenness, what spilled out was a new hunger to step into the other side of eternity. Dad had seen something, felt something, and experienced something that produced a profound understanding, which he stated simply every day. "Well, the good Lord must have something for me to do today because I'm still here!" His every purpose became wrapped up in what his Lord wanted for today. He was determined to pray more. "I don't pray enough. I need to pray more" was his repeated confession to me. After his stroke, his prayers always contained phrases about eternity. "Lord, make us ready for eternity." "We want to be with You, Lord, for eternity." "Let our family be together in eternity." He would talk about eternal purposes, eternal plans, and heavenly views. His desire to know and be part of that world was evident, if not haunting. I had no idea at the time, but I realize now that Dad had grasped the kingdom of heaven with a young child's mind. While his intellect was failing him, his spirit began to blossom. I witnessed the expansion of the kingdom of heaven and never recognized it as such. We all felt it, though. Something incredible was happening in our lives as a family and as individuals that none of us could define. I don't think it ever occurred to us to try to wrap it into words. But the kingdom of love, humility, and self-sacrifice deepened, widened, and took on solid practical form in each of our lives right here on earth. Right in the midst of what seemed to shake our very world, God's kingdom came. What did that look like? Let me expand.

As each of us gave up other plans and priorities to come together, crossing hundreds of miles and many hurdles, we learned to love deeper. We enjoyed each other's strengths and embraced one another in our weaknesses, holding one another up. We rallied around our parents, making ourselves fully available to every need and desire for those few weeks and days. We had learned to unselfishly return the love that we had received in ways that stretched us, love that had been poured out on us through the years. It had taken root in us and was now as the mustard seed that had grown into the large bush for others to enjoy and receive seed from. We had found the pearl of great value in family and love, and we now returned to the field where it was found to enjoy it. At the time, the word *enjoy* would not have crossed my mind. Looking back, however, the beautiful fragrance of what was broken and spilled out brings nothing but pleasure. It is the aroma of hearts being opened up and honest before one another. It is of precious prayer encounters together. It is of comfort given and comfort received between ones who were, just days before, worlds apart. It is of sacrificing sleep, food, and other basic comforts to keep vigil over one who kept watch over our lives. It was the aroma of a holy resignation for each and every one of us—not my will but Yours be done, Lord.

With the onset of Dad's massive stroke on April 22, 2006, the boundaries of the kingdom of heaven began to stretch out. The banks began to overflow. And what happens with an overflowing riverbank? Devastation. Destruction. Suffering. New territory is defined, covered, and established for the river. And the river is for life, cleansing, healing, freedom. In the months, weeks, and finally days leading up to Dad's departure from earth on November 22, 2006, those riverbanks expanded and grew beyond all expectation and overtook the spouses of the children, the children of the children, even the children of the children's children and numerous other friends and relatives. The kingdom of love was expanding before our very eyes without recognition.

Mom, who was now in her eighties, with us, their children now in our forties and fifties, were growing and learning through uncharted territory. Dad was leading the way. In his illness with his limited cognitive abilities, he was still coaching, teaching, and training us in the way we should go. As he hungered for the kingdom of heaven, his prayers and innocent needs paved the way for kingdom expansion. He always did enjoy building on, adding to, expanding, and improving the various homes we lived in. Dad expanded the boundaries of his tent until his last breath. His sweetness and loving demeanor taught us not to be afraid. I watched carefully and discovered that Dad had learned the secret of not being afraid. His peace and sweetness flowed from his complete dependence on the Lord Jesus Christ, his God. He had discovered that if he still had breath in his lungs, it was for the Lord. And he had no fear of heaven because then, he would be there with his Lord as well. He learned somewhere in the midst of brokenness to trust in God. "What do You want, Lord? Then that's what I'll be today." I can't say that I ever recognized that particular trait in him prior to April 22, 2006. Perhaps the Lord was working that in him, and I didn't notice. Maybe I was blind or wasn't paying attention. Nevertheless, it struck me suddenly that Dad found peace, comfort, and strength in looking to God for his purpose daily. His trials and hardship produced a brokenness that was defined by dependence on his heavenly Father. He no longer had an identity wrapped up in wood carving, golf, Knights of Columbus, the US Navy, household handyman, etc. His entire identity seemed to be wrapped up in two realms, his family on earth and his family in heaven. And Father God was central to both. Amazing.

Dad modeled that when life on earth is ebbing away, when all is said and done, what remains is God. Father God remains through our relationships with our natural family as well as our spiritual family. Dad found joy and fulfillment in both. He longed to see his children and grandchildren when we were hundreds of miles away. He took great joy in lengthy phone conversations his last months of life. He never tired of visiting when we were around him, not wanting to miss even a minute of being together. It was only his physical limitations manifested by bouts of snoring erupting in the midst of a visit that would finally force him to retreat for some rest.

Light bulbs began to come on for me. Not just one light but many. Vulnerability and weakness produced brokenness. Brokenness produced humble dependence. Dependence birthed a sweetness conceived out of the union of humility and love. And the purpose of it all was in God, for God, from God. My God, in almost twenty-five years of serving You, why hadn't I understood these truths like this before? I am so grateful that Dad had remained teachable throughout his life. It was his leading and example that allowed me to see these simple truths in living flesh and blood. Dad was raised with a foundation of faith in the church. Most of his life, he was very private about his faith, though. Only later in his life signs that Dad trusted Jesus personally as his Lord and Savior became evident. He grew in tremendous ways at the very end. What an inspiration. What motivation. To know that it matters not the condition of my body or brain. Growth is not dependent on me at all other than the simple litmus test—is my will surrendered to God's?

I wonder how many at such an age or stage of life are willing to walk in the humility it took for my dad to allow my sisters and I to sit with him countless hours working on skills like learning to read again, performing simple math functions, putting on his own shoes—things he did with us years before when we were children. What was that like for Dad? Some days I know were a struggle. Mostly, though, his attitude spoke of a desire to embrace whatever there was to embrace that day. If he felt like giving up, it was usually short-lived. Perseverance became his middle name! Why was that? How could learning to read again or performing simple math again mean that much to him at eighty-three years old? I am convinced it was because he was certain of his purpose for the day—to do that which the Lord put before him. He wanted to honor the Lord in everything. How beautiful.

This same principle of a lifelong, never-ceasing growth process taking place in the later years of one's life has been evident to me throughout the years, but never as clearly and personally demonstrated as with my own dad. I've had the privilege of sitting under the teaching of several great fathers in our faith at various conferences and meetings. What has profoundly impacted me in some of them is their humility before the Lord evidenced by fresh, new depths of revelation regarding the truths that they had read and known at a more surface level for thirty, forty, or sixty years! This has remained an inspiration to me to observe that men who have walked with Jesus for sixty or seventy years or more still have new experiences with God, have forged even deeper into that relationship with Him and have continued to grow richer and more vibrant in Him which I noticed every time I saw them. They haven't lived their lives on their successful ministry of ten years ago or the great book published fifteen years ago or the phenomenal visitation they experienced five years ago. Though those things are obviously part of them, they are each marked by a hunger and thirst for more. They are ever seeking, ever pursuing their Lord. They are great men of God who still don't consider themselves finished. Somehow, I had them set apart as special or different, though. They are God's anointed ones. They were "spiritual" men. I had come to expect that hunger and freshness from them and allowed it to spur me on.

Dad, though, he was just an ordinary man. Good ordinary— *very* good ordinary, but ordinary just the same. He didn't spend all his waking hours reading the Bible and studying. In fact, he wasn't big on reading much of anything except the sports section of the newspaper. He would labor over an occasional book if something really struck his interest, but that was far and few in between. So I never was even tempted to equate him with these great scholars in faith who taught such astounding revelation. Dad was neither a man of profound, exquisite prayers nor did I ever witness him on his knees for hours. His prayers were simple, as a conversation with one of us sitting next to him would be. In fact, I remember Mom's amusement and pleasure over some of the almost casual yet heartfelt comments Dad would make in prayer as we sat together on any given morning at the breakfast table. His simple prayers—Mom's, too, for that matter—had a way of just touching my heart in an endearing way. As I reflect on those prayers now, I can only imagine how their simple sincerity must have touched the heart of the Lord. What a sweet incense as their morning sacrifice arose to meet Jesus there in the midst of them. Nothing of great revelation or worthy of publishing in the hall of faith book—just everyday words of thanks, pleas for help, requests for blessings and provision—you know, the stuff that life is made of on a daily basis for most of us.

Dad and Mom would often take a shift each week at the chapel to help keep the twenty-four-hour chain of prayer unbroken. Perhaps this is above and beyond the average, but still it was never what I considered "great" or "earthshaking." It was simply a sign of their hunger and desire to see more of God manifested in our world. In writing now, it's so clear to me, but I missed it completely then. There it was: Mom and Dad together, their cry through an act of faith, filling an hour or two of prayer each week for their community—the fulfillment of His kingdom coming on earth as it is in heaven. Mom and Dad together praying each morning. Hungry hearts reaching into His throne room saying, "Please come, please move, please be with us now." This is what marked my dad, I believe for kingdom expansion, for a life that ended on earth so rich with God's sweet presence.

A hungry heart. Now there's something Dad had in common with those great fathers in the faith that I spoke of encountering. Somehow, I think our Father in heaven places a high value on such a quality. Jesus told us that those who hunger and thirst for righteousness will be filled. At a time in Dad's life when I said, "Enough, it's enough. He's had a good life. Let's not make things too difficult or uncomfortable for anyone here at the end, especially Mom and him. Enough," You, Lord, said, "No." Your actions proved that it was not enough. You had more. More for Dad, more for Mom, more for all of us. But who could've guessed You had so much more of Yourself to pour into an eighty-four-year-old man? And just how much more is an eighty-one-year-old woman expected to grow and absorb? Why even would such treasures of the kingdom be wasted on a nobody, no-name husband and his wife, even if it was for the good of them and their entirely insignificant, anonymous family? They were not featured anywhere in the *Hall of Faith* books nor did they occupy any positions on the platform of great preachers or infamous teachers. Why would these precious jewels of breathtaking love, glowing encouragement, sparkling intercession, radiant faith, and dazzling devotion be wasted on one who is unseen, unnoticed, unknown to the world at large? It was merely because he was hungry for the things of God—hungry for righteousness. God showed Himself faithful in this most humbling, amazing way. A simple man was hungry. He asked. God fulfilled His promise to my dad and fed him, filled him with His own righteousness, with Himself just as He said He would. These words became not *just* scripture, not just theology or biblical teaching. These words came to life, real flesh and blood life, living in my earthly dad. I watched my dad (and mom) grow in the things of God as Dad prepared for his heavenly home.

Here's the amazing part. After listening, reading, studying, praying and seeking God myself for over twenty-three years at the time, through a variety of different avenues and venues, some of the simplest, most basic truths sprang to life with new meaning, greater depth, and richer real-life application than ever before in my life. It all began to be revealed bit by bit through the heart and mind of an aged, dying, common man I called Dad. His mind had become simple. His daily accomplishments included the things most of us take for granted as not even being noteworthy at the end of our day. Simple mind. Simple life. Full spirit. Oh, how full his spirit was. He was not too old, too tired, or too spent to be filled and used of his heavenly Father. How this thought has comforted me in my mournful hours of missing my dad. More than comfort, though, an energizing, propelling encouragement remains within me as I reflect on his life lived well and full to his last breath despite his multiple limitations. Not only are the great men who are famous for their books, teachings, healing ministries, prophetic ministries, mega churches, TV, and radio programs being filled by our Father in heaven, but the insignificant are significantly filled as well. Those whom I've seen firsthand who share that same hunger who have attained significant ministries and an established name have nothing more than my dad had at the end of his days, namely, the fullness of God.

Does that stir hope in you? It should! It could if you allow it. No matter what life brings us, what condition our bodies are in, how sharp or dull our minds are, one thing we never have to forfeit is growth in the things of God. If you are hungry for righteousness, He will continue to fill you in incremental measures. It never has to end—ever. It makes no difference who you are, where you are or what you are. If you are thirsty for Him, He will give you drink that never ends from wells of living water, which become rivers of life to those around you, regardless of who they may be.

2

Holding Hands

So I have enlightened you first with the end of the story. This may be pleasing to those of you that relish skipping to the last chapter before reading a book in its entirety. I encourage you, however, don't stop here. The unfolding of the life that ended with such sweetness and love is rich with plantings in fertile soil that bore some beautiful fruit along the way. It was fruit that I had either missed or taken for granted earlier in my life. Providing pastoral care for many years in a small family-centered church, I realized in gradual stages of revelation, that I had been blessed with a family foundation of love and stability that was foreign to many. Much of what I considered "common sense" had actually been birthed from a solid traditional family. I am grateful beyond words. These next chapters will unfold some of that foundational truth that brings security and stability into a child's life. Many of us, for countless reasons, overlook these truths and step unknowingly into deception, which takes us on many of life's painful detours. It's never too late to return or to learn these truths, though, so read on!

The Beginning

When did it happen? Where did it begin? At one time, I was just an infant, helpless in every way, unable to offer anything of value to my parents except the mere being of my existence. No matter the degree of greatness attained in our lifetime, our visible net worth on a balance sheet, the magnitude of impact we make on the future of our family, community, or world, we all basically began our lives as nothing. What is it our parents or caregiver found in us that was worth pouring thankless hours of night watches, unending repetitive chores such as diapering, feeding, bathing, and all the associated mundane tasks that consume massive amounts of time, energy, and money? For what? Why? What did they get out of it? What immediate return did they receive other than perhaps a few hours of peace and quiet or an occasional gurgling smile? Perhaps it was the bond created by the thought that "this separate living being is part of me!" Others may have been motivated by the hopes and dreams of what will become of this infant one day. There are many, however, that experience great joy from that mere existence of the child in their presence. They love the way an infant snuggles in close while being held and latches her tiny fist onto her daddy's shirt to assure continued snuggling once she is fast asleep. They love to feel the soft skin and gentle breath in rhythmic ebbs and tides as he is rocked to sleep. The young eyes yet to focus with distinction warms the heart of many as those infant eyes intently study the faces of those caring for them, as if each encounter brings new discoveries. And then, of course, there's the smile, the recognition that thrills the heart of every recipient of them. For many, these simple pleasures, simple rewards of being with the infant are enough. The love and delight of the parent in the child has nothing to do with what the child can do, for the child can *do* nothing—he can only *be* a helpless child.

So then I ask, when does it happen? Where does it begin? At what point in our lives do we learn that our value to our parents (and others) comes from what we are able to do and how well we perform what we do? Perhaps this doesn't describe you at all. If not, you are in the vast minority of the population. A miniscule percentage of the human race grows up knowing that their value has nothing to do with their performance. If that's you, you may skip this chapter, though you may be intrigued by insight into how the majority of the world is motivated.

As our tiny bodies grow rapidly in infancy, we are encouraged to try new things, do new things, experience new things. We are encouraged first with gentle words, smiles, hugs, and pleasant little pats or rubs. We have a natural positive response to relational rewards. As we continue to grow, however, materialistic rewards are introduced as positive reinforcement and punishments or joy-shattering disapproval is introduced as negative reinforcements. Behaviors are taught or discouraged in this way, and we learn to perform according to expectations. Unfortunately, without regular doses of unconditional affirmation based on who or what the child is outside of their performance, a very young child quickly makes the connection that love and acceptance has everything to do with what they *do*, and *who* they are is of little consequence. As the parents' expectation of their sweet little child changes and grows, often, so does the message of unconditional love. The more critical and demanding the parent is, the more performance based the child becomes. If a parent is attentive to provide love and affirmation outside of the regular times of training and discipline, a child is more confident in their value and less likely to engage in attention seeking behaviors, both negative and positive. Most children grow up getting the idea of "The better I perform, the more I'll be loved." It is a human nature kind of response. It is in fact a sinful kind of response birthed from the first act of doubt and disobedience in the Garden of Eden in the beginning of man's days. It is part of the curse over all mankind.

You may be wondering how. What's the connection? Consider the account of God's creation of man and then immediately following the creation in Genesis 2:7–9, 15–17.

> The Lord God formed the man from the dust of the ground and breathed into his nostrils the breath of life, and the man became a living being. Now the Lord God had planted a garden in the east, in Eden; and there he put the man he had formed. And the Lord God made all kinds of trees grow out of the ground—trees that were pleasing to the eye and good for food. In the mid-

> dle of the garden were the tree of life and the tree
> of the knowledge of good and evil… The Lord
> God took the man and put him in the Garden of
> Eden to work it and take care of it. And the Lord
> God commanded the man, "You are free to eat
> from any tree in the garden; but you must not eat
> from the tree of the knowledge of good and evil,
> for when you eat of it you will surely die."

Note that the man was given the work of caring for the garden. He was also given every provision for food within the garden with the one restriction. According to Genesis 1:26, God created mankind and only mankind in his own image with the authority to rule over all other species and the whole earth. He commanded them to be fruitful and increase in number in Genesis 2:28. The entire account implies an air of superior value given to Adam and Eve. Though they are given responsibility and authority in the earth, there are no conditions on their position. One and only one condition is mentioned: "for when you eat of it [the tree of good and evil] you will surely die."

We all know the story, and of course, they did eat. Though death was not immediate, it was eminent. The immediate consequences, however, were twofold. First of all, there was an awareness of good vs. evil. Before, they only perceived good. Suddenly, after eating of the knowledge of good and evil, there came an understanding that some things may be evil, such as nakedness, which was previously completely innocent. This indicates that not that nakedness was suddenly wrong, but that their minds were now awakened to perversity, shame, and guilt. In this state came the response to hide who they really were with what they could do, covering themselves with fig leaves. The second related consequence was that the entire nature of their work changed. They were removed from the garden so they would not be allowed any longer to eat from the tree of life and live forever, and they were placed under a curse that changed their working of the land into painful toil and pain in reproducing.

Understand now what this means. We are all born as innocent, helpless infants into mankind under a curse of painful works, needing to learn the difference between good and evil. Our tendency now is toward perverse perceptions (or twisted if you will from the original purity it was created in as with the example of nakedness and Adam and Eve). We have the ability to see the evil side of things and, with our free will, can easily choose evil over good. Our work throughout life does not come with the pleasure and ease of the Garden of Eden but now carries with it sweat and pain. This is the natural state we are born into, which we grow into and are led into.

Do you get it? This sets the stage for a child to naturally perceive that even though he knew his parents' love and acceptance from birth, he gravitates toward feeling that he must work for love, for his sustenance. She knows good, but she has an awareness of evil and is tempted to explore that as well, requiring discipline to direct her into goodness, further reinforcing a behavior based acceptance and love.

The most unfortunate thing about this human response is that it has nothing to do with how our heavenly Father feels about us. Though there are rewards for good behavior both on earth and eternally, as well as punishments for bad or disobedient behavior, He *always* loves us. In fact, even though Adam and Eve's original act of disobedience resulted in a sinful mankind under a curse of works, God loved us while we were still sinners, and He loves us as He continues to forgive us throughout our lives. He loved us so much that He sent Jesus, His Son, to die for us and pay the price for our sin. That act of obedience on Jesus's part resulted in His resurrection, showing the ultimate victory over the death curse over us. All we need to do is believe it and accept it. Part of the beauty and joy of the garden for Adam and Eve was the close fellowship they had with God. They walked with him in the cool of the day. They met with Him, talked to Him, and spent time with Him.

The thing about love, God's love, is that it requires relationship. It's more than the "doing" kind of relationship. Again, the parent of the newborn loves her not because of what she does, but because she's theirs. In pure parental love, this never changes, even though the message the child receives or interprets often does. It might seem like an elementary truth to know that we are loved unconditionally, but the vast majority of us don't really believe it in our hearts. My husband loves to quote one his favorite sayings that "if you raise the dead or take a nap, God loves you just the same." Do we believe it? I had heard the message of unconditional love and how our heavenly Father just wants us to *be* with Him for many years. I have read it, said it, taught it, and tried to live it by spending regular times alone with God; but it was only as my own earthly father became weak and disabled that I really began to grasp it.

For years, I loved traveling the 1,800 miles to visit my parents by myself at least once a year. As one of seven children in my family, I was hard-pressed to remember spending individual time with either of my parents. This time, alone with them as an adult was really a time of getting to know them in a new way, one-on-one, in deeper relationship. It was a time I put great value on and wouldn't trade for anything. Going and spending time there felt like heaven to me—a peaceful resting place of sweet fellowship. Though building a deeper relationship with Mom and Dad was the goal for me, I always went with an agenda of what I could do for them. Though I was comfortable and at peace with them when I went, I still always had this nagging "what can I *do* for them?" sensation undergirding everything. Sometimes I went specifically to assist them during times of rehab following an illness or medical procedure. Sometimes I went down just to go, but I still always would tell them "Make your list of things you want done, and I'll do it!" Though I knew that my parents valued my visits regardless of my accomplishments for them, my heart somehow still clung to that concept that they would enjoy or appreciate me more if I could just do something for them. Now it is good to care enough about others to give of your time and energy in serving them. Jesus taught us to serve others and do good works. The point I'm making, however, is that this is not the basis for love. After twenty-two years of being a Christian and probably eight or more years of annual visits alone with my parents, I still had not fully grasped the value of the love outside of the works.

Not until April 23, when my world come to a screeching halt and was turned inside out for seven months. The call came just afternoon on the busiest day of the week for me—Sunday. In the middle of a churchwide potluck dinner for a missionary friend from Russia, my sister finally reached me, frantic, to let me know that Dad had a massive stroke and wasn't expected to live to see tomorrow. My first thought was immediate guilt. I had been putting off a visit to them earlier in the year despite a nagging feeling that I needed to go. Finally, I had listened and scheduled a visit, but it wasn't until the following week. Why hadn't I listened to the Holy Spirit? That had to have been Him trying to tell me that time was short with my dad. Now I feared it was too late to ever see him alive. I was filled with anguish and regrets as my mind raced to try to figure out what needed to be done to make it to Dad. Within just a few hours, my only sister that lived nearby and I were at the airport together, headed to Florida. I agonized in prayer, not knowing how to pray. About two years before I had asked the Lord during one of my visits for the gift of being with my parents when they pass into eternity. I viewed it as such a precious thing that I had an intense desire to experience that with them each. When I asked the Lord for this, I had no idea how He would be able to work that out for me since I live 1,800 miles away, but I trusted that if He wanted, He could, in fact, work out such details.

Now, in waiting for my flight, I wondered if Dad was suffering. If so, it would be selfish for me to ask for him to be kept alive until I got there. Or at age eighty-three, should I pray for his healing? Was God ready to gather him unto Himself, or did Dad have more ahead yet on earth? Was Mom ready to let go or did she need more time? Would his life be miserable and full of suffering if he lived? If so, maybe I should pray for God to take Him quickly now, even if it meant forfeiting my once-in-a-lifetime opportunity to be with him in his passing. I was confused. I was filled with guilt and misery at the thought of possibly having missed seeing Dad alive again because I'd procrastinated in scheduling my visit. My prayers took on the form of complete resignation, asking for God's best, for His mercy, for His grace for us all to endure whatever was ahead.

Then I would switch back to pleading for Dad to live at least so I could see him one last time. Ultimately, my desire to be with Dad won out over and over again as I wrestled in prayer all the way to Florida. Upon our arrival to the hospital, we were much relieved to see Dad was hanging on. In the first attempt of countless times ahead, I caressed my dad's hand and then carefully, cautiously held it in mine. I don't remember if Dad was able to communicate even a groan at this point, but I do remember being grateful to just be there beside him, touching him, feeling the warmth of the little life still within him. Over the span of the next week, Dad's awareness of us, his family and beloved wife increased gradually, though his ability to communicate or comprehend his surroundings was extremely limited. My mom, my siblings, and various grandchildren kept twenty-four-hour vigils at his bedside.

I remember when it happened, when the revelation hit me. It was about two o'clock one morning as I kept watch next to Dad in his hospital bed. I was holding his hand—now limp and soft and yet the strength that this hand once knew was evident in its size and tone. Dad was sleeping soundly, peacefully, or so I thought. All was quiet. So I very gently, carefully slipped my hand out from underneath his to change my position and move about a bit and it happened. The revelation exploded within my spirit as I witnessed Dad reach for me, feebly stretching out to the edge of the bed. The revelation came that Dad was enjoying my presence with him, even though neither us of had spoken. I had not performed any of the comforting rituals, which my three professional nurse sisters and mom so skillfully provided at regular intervals. I was just there, sometimes quietly praying, but mostly just quietly there, holding his hand. I had no idea he was really aware of it. I didn't know it really mattered to him. I had hoped it did but couldn't be sure. Now I knew for sure; he knew I was there, he wanted me there, and he wanted me touching him, holding his hand. My being there meant something to him. I didn't matter because of what I was doing. It was my touch, the assurance of my presence that mattered, that ministered to him. I began to really grasp that it wasn't the "doing" for Dad that was important to him. It was the "being" that mattered more than anything. Previously I had struggled over and over with lack of value compared to my sisters and mom who knew what to do, how to do it, when to do it. They communicated in what seemed like a foreign language with the doctors so that my head literally ached from trying to understand. I was of no use to my dad at this stage of his life. I desperately wanted to do something and be of help, but my inadequacies were glaring. Now, though, tonight, I realized that it didn't matter to Dad because *I* mattered to Dad.

The Holy Spirit began then to open my eyes to the fact that this is how it is with our heavenly Father. What we are able to perform, the skills we have, the level of communication present is not nearly as important to Him as the fact that we are present with Him. More than anything, He wants us to come to Him, sit with Him, hold His hand. This was my first glimpse into what was meant by Jesus when He spoke to busy, worried, resentful Martha "Only one thing is needed. Mary has chosen what is better, and it will not be taken away from her." What Mary had chosen was to sit at the feet of Jesus, listening to Him. The Lord was saying it's our being next to Him that is His desire.

Consider for a moment, the act of holding hands. Children do it with their parents as a form of protection, guidance, or reassurance. They hold one another's hands in play or innocent, sincere, close friendship. Lovers do it out of deep affection and a desire to remain literally in touch with one another. Adults rarely hold hands with another unless there is some kind of intimate relationship. Sometimes people will join hands in prayer or as a group to make a public statement of some sort as a means to show unity. Mostly, however, holding hands is reserved for children or lovers. It speaks of vulnerability or intimacy. Perhaps this is why when describing the beautiful experience of holding my dad's hand to a friend one day, she looked at me with an expression that indicated she could not imagine it could be anything but awkward. It was precious to me, however, because it broke a barrier into a new depth of closeness that Dad and I had not yet experienced. At age forty-seven, he valued me as his daughter, just because I was his, and he loved having me beside him. It is this kind of intimate and even protective love that our heavenly Father has for us, His precious children. In fact, it is this kind of love, only increased exponentially. Psalm 139 takes on deeper personal meaning knowing how much our Father loves to be with us. It says that He hems us in from the front and back, and He has lovingly laid His hand upon us. There is no place we can go to flee from Him. His hand is on us wherever we go to guide us. His right hand holds us fast. We can see this clearly in the scriptures.

> You hem me in—behind and before, you have laid your hand upon me. Where can I go from your Spirit? Where can I flee from your presence? If I go up to the heavens, you are there; if I make my bed in the depths, you are there. If I rise on the wings of the dawn, if I settle on the far side of the sea, even there your hand will guide me, your right hand will hold me fast. (Psalm 139:5, 7, 10)

Return to the thought of holding hands—an intimate, protective imagery. This is the kind of relationship our Father desires with each one of us. It is only awkward if we are distant and uncomfortable in our relationship with Him.

Take it one step further. Think of the young child who loves to be up on her daddy's lap, peacefully resting her head on his chest, snuggled in close. There is no agenda, no to-do list, just the pleasure of sitting close together. Or think of the toddler who loves to be carried through the mall even though they have the ability to walk, and there is a stroller readily available as well. It's the being close to mom or dad that is the main point—nothing else is important. Can we consider ourselves in that place with our heavenly Father, where it's the closeness, being in His Presence that counts? It's what counts most to Him. He sent His one and only Son Jesus, to die so that we could be close and no one could snatch us out of His hand (John 10:28–29).

Though He created works for each of us to do in our lives, He made our entrance into His presence dependent not on the work we perform, but the faith that we have, and even that was a gift from Him that we can simply choose to believe or not. There is no one disabled or limited in any way that cannot perform the simple exercise of faith to enter into His rest and peace He has for us. It's so simple that even children are able to grasp and hold onto it—His hand if you will. Faith is as His hand that He holds out to us and through this faith He is with us always. He never leaves us, never forsakes us. Once we have chosen Him, His hand is forever on us. Only we ourselves can release ourselves from His grasp. We can never be tricked, snatched, or stolen away. When we begin to inch away or get distracted from Him, He reaches out for us to hang on and draw us back to Him, just as my dad did that night. I remember how my heart ached with love for Dad at the thought that he had pursued me with his hand the second I released him.

Again, this is a perfect picture of Father God. He is so aware of our every move and every thought (Psalm 139:1–4). If we ever are obstinate and rebellious and determine to break free from His grasp, He pursues us just as the Shepherd searches for the lost lamb. He watches and prepares for our return as He did for the prodigal. These examples are again proof that He is willing to pursue and forgive because our presence with Him is everything! Being together is the point. The rewards or crowns we earn with our actions are all for one purpose anyway, to lay before Him in heavenly worship (Revelation 4:9–10). So even still, it's all about being with Him. My point—staying connected, touching Him, being in His Presence *is* the point. *Presence* is what matters above and beyond all else.

I'm reminded of an encounter about six months after Dad's stroke when I had flown in for a few days to sit with him while others moved my parents to a home they were planning to share with my sister and brother in-law. In my dad's childlike mental state and weakened physical condition, there were many precious moments riddled with challenges as well. I treasured every moment with him that few days, however, perceiving that his time left would be very short. Leaving to return home began to feel unbearably difficult as I considered the possibility of not seeing him again where he was still able to recognize me. After I hugged and kissed him one last time in his recliner, I walked across the room toward the door, my heart in agony over my departure. I turned at the door to look at him one last time so this picture of "dear old dad" (his favorite way to refer to himself) could be etched in my memory forever. I drank in the image and his voice, which caused my heart to shatter in a thousand pieces, exploding with a yearning to stay. I saw his brow furrowed and mouth pouting out the words he spoke to my mom in such childlike innocence, "Gee, I wish she could stay!" I turned quickly, leaving to hide the tears that refused to be held back any longer as he obediently lifted his hand, that treasured hand, to wave one last goodbye, which I returned all too hastily.

My heart was not made to say goodbye to Dad. Our hearts were made for eternity. We were designed for eternal life, eternal fellowship, and eternal relationship. Leaving Dad that day was one of the hardest things I have ever done. And this is what our heavenly Father desires for us—constant fellowship. It's clear in John's writing that Jesus intends to take us to be with Him forever as He assures the disciples in John 14:3, "I will come back and take you to be with me that you also may be where I am."

Furthermore, He says that He will be with us always now through His Holy Spirit in John 14:16–17a, "And I will ask the Father, and he will give you another Counselor to be with you forever—the Spirit of truth." We need to choose to remain with Him, however, as He challenged His followers in John 15:5 saying, "I am the vine; you are the branches. If a man remains in me and I in him, he will bear much fruit; apart from me you can do nothing." His heart breaks when we leave His presence just as my dad and I experienced our hearts breaking that last day I left him in his recliner. The challenge for us is to find that place with Him in relationship where we are always conscious of Him, attentive to His presence always.

I have reflected often remembering my dad's hand—his warmth, softness, gentle strength; and it is a contact point for a picture of my Father God in heaven. It brings me comfort, warmth, and peace because I know Father God's hand never leaves me because I belong to Him. I'm His daughter and He's my Abba (Daddy) who loves me with Him, not because of what I do, but because of who I am—His.

3

Favorite One

In speaking of how much our heavenly Father loves to be with us, some of us say in our hearts, "Maybe, but there are others that are more important to Him than me." Another lesson learned—there's no truth in that thought. Throughout the years on earth with my dad, he made something very clear to my young heart. It became clear to the hearts of my siblings at various stages of life, some much later than others. The message that came from our heavenly Father through the earthly vessel of my dad was this: We are all highly valued, even to the point of saying we each are his favorite. Let me explain.

Dad had a way with us that I never really fully appreciated until late in life. I never recognized it as a child, but I realize now, as a seasoned parent myself, how beautifully divine this characteristic was. You see, Dad had a way of making each of us feel special. Think of it—six daughters and one son—seven children in all, and all of us knew his favor by the end of his life. Though Dad was far from perfect and had his shortcomings in parenting like we all do, by the time his life on earth ended, each one of us knew how cherished and valued we were by him. We each knew we held a uniquely special place in his heart shared by not one of the others. Each of us were as though we were his one and only favorite. In fact, quite possibly, if you were to catch any of us alone, confidentially, and ask, "Who was your dad's favorite child?" I'm guessing that each would secretly confess independently "I am!" I began to ponder this and realize this trait was somewhat unique in earthly fathers.

As I reflected further, watching him interact with each one of us as his body was giving way to his last days on earth, I realized his deep love and affection for each of my siblings just as he had shown me. I observed, deeply touched, by the extent of love and tenderness bestowed on each family member almost every time there was an encounter. My dad had come to a place where he embraced and cherished each of us with the same gentle touch, the same patriarchal blessing of love and gratitude that made us know we were loved, accepted, and held dear to him. He made us know our value to him, like we truly were his rewards (Psalms 127:3), his joy and delight (Proverbs 23:24).

I wondered how he managed to have seven children *all* who honored him and loved him so without alienating even one. How had he lived out in us Song of Songs 6:9, which refers to all of us as the chosen ones of Christ, considering us individuals as a unique, favorite one? How did he so beautifully celebrate us as his reward, his joy and delight?

It was a characteristic of Father God that I had not understood very clearly before. I knew Father loved me, but it would be quite arrogant to imagine that He loved me the same as Moses, David, John, Paul, or Billy Graham even. Weren't they greater? Weren't they worthy of more love? Weren't their historical works of faith, love, and sacrifice looked upon with greater favor that would solicit greater delight? Though their heavenly rewards may be great, the scriptures indicate that we are all embraced with the same love and draw the same exuberant response from our Father as He rejoices with singing over each of us (Zephaniah 3:17). Yet I couldn't believe or receive it until I felt this trait radiate with great tenderness from Dad. Just what was it that caused us to know this kind of favored love?

I began to see how my dad had unknowingly instilled unique value at a young age. He had bestowed on each one of us a special nickname. Names are important. Biblical accounts of various names reflect the character or traits of the individual. The book of Genesis is filled with account after account of names given which describe the ones born. Abram's name was changed to *Abraham* to reflect his covenant with God. Jacob's name changed to Israel after wrestling with the Lord. Though all of us Schuhler children had been given carefully selected names at birth, my dad lovingly dubbed us each at some point with a special name that was his way of special affection toward us. Our nicknames reflected some endearing trait or displayed his playful joy in us. Our nicknames were always used affectionately in times of fun but were never used in anger or discipline. These names reflected only the positive, encouraging, fun side of our relationship with Dad.

To this day, I can sense only the warmth of Dad's playful love as I hear his voice calling out to his "Perky" (my cherished nickname). The name was used in cherished moments that made me feel set apart, singled out as one especially dear to him. There was never a time in my life that Dad ever stopped using my name in an endearing way. Nor did Dad ever stop using the childish, yet completely precious name he'd chosen just for me. He was still calling me Perky through his last days. It was part of my identity with Dad.

Dad's name for me secretly remained an encouragement to me throughout my adult life. I went through times when I didn't feel very "Perky," but it resonated in me, refusing to die because it had been spoken over me so much by my father. There were times when I felt ridiculed, criticized, misunderstood because of my energy and ambition. In these times, I was subconsciously encouraged because I understood from my nickname as a child that this was a trait my father cherished. He enjoyed my "perkiness." Being appreciated by my dad somehow made the rest easier. Having been given a special name reserved just for Dad and me somehow built a value and worth in my soul that remained with me throughout many difficult, rocky times in life.

It didn't occur to me until just recently, though, why. This is something that our heavenly Father does for us. Isaiah 62:2–3 says, "You will be called by a new name that the mouth of the Lord will bestow. You will be a crown of splendor in the Lord's hand, a royal diadem in the hand of your God." And Revelation 3:12 says, "And I will also write on him my new name."

Our heavenly Father has a new name for each of us as we are born into Him just as He did for Abraham, Sarah, Israel, Paul, and Peter. Our new name reflects that beautifully unique, valuable character within us that steals His heart and causes Him to look upon us as the favorite child. Each of us hold a special place in His heart that no other can fill or even touch. There is a place in Him for only this child and no other. He looks upon each of us as the glorious royal crown in His hand. No two crowns are alike, and each is as beautiful and valuable to Him as the other. Consider the thought that *you* are His favorite beautiful crown that He holds in His hand to gaze upon and enjoy. The king may have many crowns, each one inlaid with unique precious jewels and stones in unique settings, shapes and sizes, therefore reflecting the light, His light, in a unique manner. The king doesn't have a favorite crown but fully appreciates and enjoys the beauty of every single crown in all its glorious radiance of color and brightness.

So we are. We have such varied combinations of characteristics and gifting, placed so lovingly deliberately within us that each one is a masterpiece. As He looks over each one within His hand, He refuses to choose one over the other as they are all beautiful. Each produces such a delight and thrill of joy within His heart that it is as His favorite, just as the others around it are. Can you fathom that you are the king's *favorite* child? There is no other like you for Him, none that can take your place in His heart.

My dad had another way of emphasizing this point. I knew my brother, as the only son, had a special place in the family—a treasured place of honor. Yet Dad never allowed any of his daughters to feel they were of lesser value. At times, he made it clear we were challenges to him, but we knew our high value as we were each referred to as "dearest daughter," and then he would attach the order number. I was dearest daughter no. 5. I was his one and only no. 5 daughter, and I was very dear to him. I held a position as daughter no. 5 that no one else had, nor could they ever. Only recently did I discover the significance in my heart of Dad's playful references to his dearest daughter. This is, however, so like our heavenly Father. Each of us were born in that unique time and place that can never be repeated or duplicated. *You* will never be replaced. Not only that, beyond the ability of my dad or any other, our heavenly Father specifically *chose* to form you and bring you into existence, destined to be His favorite one. He created your inmost being in your mother's womb in the most glorious, wonderful way (Psalm 139:13–14).

Do you need further proof of how valuable you are as His favorite one? Just think for a moment of one that you love dearly. Are they not often, even constantly in your thoughts? Psalm 139:17–18 further says, "How precious [concerning] me are Your thoughts, O God! How vast is the sum of them! Were I to count them, they would outnumber the grains of the sand." How many grains of sand are in a handful? Can you count even that miniscule portion?

One day, as I walked the great white expanse of the Gulf Coast shoreline, I was pondering this very thought, "Your thoughts, Lord, toward me outnumber the grains of sand…really?" I gazed across the dunes to my left and the endless beach stretched before me. It wasn't until I looked down and considered counting the miniscule granules lightly coating my feet like freshly baked sugar cookies. The realization washed over me as though one of the breakers had knocked me over, that it was much farther beyond comprehension than I had ever fathomed. I became completely overwhelmed with the contemplation that not only do God's thoughts for me outnumber the sand, but for everyone else that has ever lived as well! I couldn't even begin to count the miniscule portion scattered on my feet, much less on this beach. That's not even considering the rest of the deserts and beaches or pockets of sandy terrain in the world! I felt my mind wanting to explode! Then I began to consider this concept in light of eternity, how our Father had no father of His own because He has always existed. Our Father will continue on forever as well, with no end. Only in light of eternity could I continue to think of His thoughts toward me. This further exemplifies the height and depth of His love, though.

Consider one that you dearly loved but has deceased. Do you ever stop thinking of them completely? Memories of my own dad pepper my days regularly, even after many years of being separated from him by death. Our Father has forever to continue thinking of us. Consider also that He also thought of us long before we were born, into eternity past, as suggested by Psalm 139:16, "Your eyes saw my unformed body. All the days ordained for me were written in Your book before one of them came to be." Couple that with the thousands of prophecies in the scriptures concerning individuals, people groups and eras, and there is no question that our Father not only thinks of us but also *knows* us well before birth, reaching into the depths of eternity past. The Father's thoughts toward you are more than we can *begin* to fathom! He was not surprised by my mistakes, my sin, my failures. In spite of it all, He loves me as His favorite child.

Father loves *you*. *You* are His favorite child. He delights in you like no other. With thoughts toward you numbering greater than the grains of sand, it may be even appropriate to say He is obsessed with you as a parent is consumed with that precious only child. Dare to believe it. Open your heart to it. Let the warmth and comfort of this truth transform your heart!

4

The Coach

Dad had a love for sports. Particularly, Dad had a passion for football—American, full-contact, tackle football. It was a puzzlement to me as a daughter because as such a gentle, kind man, the thrill he received from a good tackle or the fight through the line of defense to make the touchdown seemed contrary to his nature. Inside, he had this tough, "go for it, fight for it" nature that seemed to only surface through football.

As a boy, he had to sneak and manipulate to play on the school team. His own father discouraged him from wasting his time and energy on such things, ignoring the strengths in his son and the joy he received from the game. Dad's mom, though, caught a glimpse of her son's heart and couldn't bear to see him crushed. She secretly would sign the papers required to play.

It turned out that Dad was quite good at football. He was strong. He was motivated. He worked hard at it. And he loved it. He developed a dream of becoming a coach for other young men needing encouragement, training, and who wanted to express themselves through the game. He received a full-ride scholarship for college to play football. It looked like, despite his own father's attempts to drown the dream, Dad's hope of becoming a coach would become a reality.

Unfortunately, as Dad entered college, World War II was brewing, and after just one season of play, one brief semester of college, he was drawn away by his sense of duty and loyalty and joined the US Navy—never to return to college again.

Growing up, we were all aware of Dad's unfulfilled dream. Periodically, he would mention with a heavy heart, how, yeah, he always wanted to be a football coach. He would never really complain about it as he rationalized that other things just ended up being more important and got in the way. First it was the war. Then it was providing a home for his new wife after the war. Then the children began to come along at close intervals. Life responsibilities got in the way, and with no encouragement from anyone to follow his dream, it remained only a dream. Dad fell into a life of doing whatever he could to provide for the endless needs of the growing family—seven children in all. And not one played football. No one entered into Dad's dream to help him play it out. It always made me kind of sad to think of.

I began to realize, though, in reflecting over Dad's life, that God had given him such a gift of encouragement that it just couldn't be held back. It became obvious to me that in reality, Dad had been a coach after all, a life coach. And I realized that, from two completely different perspectives, it was a beautiful display of our heavenly Father's love being played out in the field of Dad's life.

From the standpoint of Dad's gifting, the real person that God created him to be, whether it happened on the football field or in the mundane fields of daily life, Dad was a great coach. He had that gift to encourage, to spur others on. He also had the ability to discern what was needed and was often wise in that discernment and the direction or counsel that resulted. He often was not listened to or followed, but his abilities were nevertheless evident. The fact that of seven children, all grown with families of their own, all seven were still close to Dad at his death, with none of us having separated ourselves from him for any length of time, was living proof of Dad's life-coach skills. God didn't allow Dad's gifts to go untapped or undeveloped even though he lacked the formal education. They merely took on a different form. God was faithful to develop and use what my dad chose for his life, even though it didn't look like what he'd envisioned. God was faithful to perform His purpose in spite of the lack of encouragement given to my dad. It was in spite of wars. It was in spite of the responsibilities of life that weighed heavy. God still caused his gifts to blossom and flower so that those around him could enjoy his fragrance—the fragrance of Christ.

God is not bound in any way nor are His Almighty hands tied by our well-meaning choices. Many of us fret over making the right choices or grieve over lost opportunities in life. We worry and sweat over the decisions before us, fearful of displeasing our Father with the wrong choice. The truth is, however, that our heavenly Father is honored when we make any decision with His will in mind. He's not trying to trick us to see how devoted we are or hide from us to see how well we persevere. He gifted us with a free will to make choices concerning what we do with the unique package of talents, strengths, and weaknesses we were each designed with from birth. He expects us to exercise that free will throughout the entirety of life, knowing that, at times, we will make mistakes or sometimes make choices that cost us our dreams. Our heavenly Father is faithful, though, to step in at those places of life and watch over the things He planted and for those that love Him and desire to follow Him, He weaves His grace and mercy into the circumstances of our lives to make sure those things that began the dreams in the first place get watered, take root, and grow. Often this is in spite of the things we've chosen for ourselves.

I can look back on my dad's life and see that he could have made it through college and been a great coach if he hadn't been so concerned about providing that first home for my mom and infant siblings. His earning potential would have been better in the long run as well. God doesn't look at what was missed, though. He looks at the opportunities still ahead. God honored the decisions my dad made based on his concern for providing for his family by causing those teaching strengths and gifts of encouragement to come through his parenting of his children, in-law children, grandchildren, and staff at work. He was a guide for neighboring kids and church youth and park board and recreation participants. Instead of his gifts being focused on a select few young men, God was faithful to cause that gift to grow in whatever arena Dad was involved in. Father God

Himself coached the coach, nurturing the planting in his life at every stage.

Sometimes I wonder if Dad felt as though he had fallen short or even failed. I'm certain he had a sense of disappointment in some ways, which played out in his great obsession with watching football and becoming completely absorbed in the game no matter who was playing. I realized late in his life how truly faithful God had been to activate that dream of his. My only regret is that I was unable to relay that to him earlier, as I believe it would have provided comfort and joy to his heart. Anyway, God had not allowed Dad's dream to die as he remained active coaching his children and many others around him through life. This was God's faithfulness revealed.

The other perspective, though, pertains to the way Dad became a life coach. In reflecting on just how he encouraged and trained others, I saw so much of our Father God revealed.

I remember Dad always being somewhat particular about how he wanted things done. He would allow a degree of flexibility at times in the approach or method but never in the finished product. He would give direction, often with a demonstration. He was very clear about the expected outcome or end results. Then he would step aside and allow you to make the attempt, all the while watching over you. There were times I could see he would really want to step in and take over but would restrain himself. He would watch, though—carefully, closely—almost too closely! He would provide correction or additional direction when he felt it was needed but always in an encouraging manner. He was never overly demanding, cruel, or demeaning about his correction and direction. It was given in such a way that would make you want to keep at it or try again. It was always a joy to me to work with my dad. Whether we were gardening together, working on a remodeling project, taking care of the lawn, or even preparing a box for shipping it was a good experience.

Several things stand out in my mind as dad coached me through life.

- He was clear about his expectations.
- He had high expectations, but they were attainable.

- He provided words of encouragement along the way.
- He observed but didn't interfere unless correction was needed.
- It was clear when you hit the mark accompanied by much affirmation and praise.

Not all my siblings always shared this same experience with my dad, but it was his greatest strength to me. It stands out so vividly because I believe that God our Father wanted me to perceive that this is how *He* is with us. He is our life coach.

Through the scriptures and our interactions with Him, Father clearly lays out His expectations. He even gives us tips or guidelines on how to be successful in living them out. He tells us things like how to pray (Matthew 6, 1 Thessalonians 5:17, Romans 8:26), how to maintain a good attitude (Philippians 4:8–9), how to treat one another, how to treat our parents and children, how to get through trials, etc. He clearly defines the essence of the things that please Him such as faith and love. He provides the equipment and help that we need to play in the game of life through His Word and His Holy Spirit. He provides correction and demonstration through the same and through those around us. He is always providing encouragement, cheering us on to try again. He spurs us on to continue if we allow ourselves to listen. It comes when we look to Him and seek Him. He constantly affirms us through His love, saying, "That's it! Keep going. I'm right with you. We'll do it together—come on now! It might be rough right now, but you're not crushed! Your opponent hasn't won. Let's give it another go!"

What I love most is that Father always affirms us in the attempts and doesn't expect immediate perfection. He gives us one play at a time, one exercise at a time until we're ready to take the field. Then, when we're worn out, exhausted, discouraged or beat up and injured, He pulls us back, revives us, heals us, and gives us the courage and strength to go again. He requires us to play the game as part of the whole team and teaches us to work together depending on one another's strengths and helping each other's weaknesses. He's right in there with us, active, remaining close, never abandoning us. That's called grace. It means that He's an interactive coach, giving us what we need when we need it, never too soon and never too late. He's not just a careful observer but He gives freely of Himself. He gives not something outside of Himself, but He gives *Himself*, through His Holy Spirit, through His Son Jesus. If we are struggling to love, He gives Himself through His Spirit because He *is* love. If we are struggling with patience or kindness or forgiveness, He gives Himself because love defined in 1 Corinthians 13 *is* all these things. If we need wisdom, He gives of Himself because the book of Proverbs shows all throughout that He *is* wisdom. And so it continues for every other need. He *is* all-powerful, the Almighty, so strength is His. He is the Prince of peace, so peace also is Him. He goes the extra mile beyond external coaching to fill us with Himself, through His Holy Spirit, so that He does His coaching from within. Jesus explains this so beautifully to His disciples in John 14–17, the night before He went to the cross. He described it as sending a "counselor" or "comforter"—the person that would come in His place to lead, direct, remind…or "coach" us through life.

This should bring us great comfort and encouragement to know that before Jesus went to the cross, He and the Father had it all taken care of. They provided the best possible life coach, even far better than my dad, to work within us forever, never leaving us. My dad had to leave, but the Holy Spirit never does.

The best part is that our coach, the Holy Spirit, has everything that the Father and Son have. He's just waiting for the right moments in life to show us, teach us, to speak. Many people don't understand the Holy Spirit or, worse yet, are afraid of Him. He is not One to be feared but to be embraced! He has every answer we could ever need. He fills every gap because He is able, He is Spirit. He knows the Father perfectly, knows us perfectly, and is the One who brings us together perfectly. Ignoring the Holy Spirit is rejecting the greatest, most perfect coach in all of history and in all the ages to come. It is to entrust yourself to less qualified, less effective, imperfect voices of the world's ways or even our enemy. Do you want the opposing team's coach speaking and directing you? That would be unheard of! It would be an obvious violation.

I learned through my good dad here on earth that Father God desires to coach us through our lives in a most positive, encouraging, interactive way. He provided His Holy Spirit to do this. If you haven't opened your life to the Holy Spirit, avoid Him no more! He is the greatest coach you will ever experience. If you already have a relationship with Him, keep going! Keep listening! Keep following! Don't be afraid of His corrections or His direction. It may seem hard at times or maybe even impossible. Be assured of this, though. He has your best future in His heart and is ready to take you there Himself!

5

The Sacrificial Life

Sacrifice. It's not a popular term. We don't like to think about it. What does it really mean? In this day and age of instant everything, electronics and mechanics to assist in everything, purchasing power to buy whatever we need (if not everything we want), the world is at our fingertips. Then, when relationships become difficult, we dispose of those too and move ourselves out and on to new ones. We can even move to methods of interacting with others that requires little or no risk of true personal interaction or giving through the use of email, texting, interactive internet cultures, and video games. People fall in love or forge "deep" relationships across the world without having ever spent even a moment of time together face-to-face, without making even a single move from the comfort of their cushy couch or computer chair in their home. We frown upon giving up our personal comforts more and more the farther we move into the twenty-first century.

Sacrifice. It's one of those words that I wonder about the meaning. Does it even have the same meaning as it did one hundred years ago, or two hundred or two thousand? Is it one of those words going through a metamorphosis of meaning? Take *gay* for example. In 1900, a pastor could proclaim from the pulpit that he was feeling quite gay and the congregation would know he was in good spirits, filled with the joy of the Lord. Today, if he proclaimed the same, there might be a huge uproar from the congregation of how the pastor is struggling with a sinful lifestyle and should be removed as a result until he can get himself straight again. In other words, what does it mean when we are called to sacrificial lifestyle? In Old Testament days, it meant bringing your lamb, ram, grain, cakes, or other specified offering to suit the occasion to the priest to be prepared in the appropriate way before the Lord on the altar. New Testament teaching speaks of giving all that we have (the widow and the mite, the rich young man, the early church that sold property to care for the widows and orphans). Father God gave His most precious possession—His Son—as a sacrifice. Jesus gave His very life as a sacrifice. He gave up having a home, a wife, natural children, property, livestock, and anything else that had any earthly value in His day.

What defines sacrifice today? Is it giving up that coffee shop hazelnut latte this week to put a few dollars in the mission's jar? Is it giving up your night at home in front of the TV to go to the prayer meeting? Is it getting to church forty-five minutes early so you can be a greeter at the door this week? Is it staying awake for an hour in the middle of the night on occasion when the Lord asks you to pray? Is it walking out of your comfort zone across the street to greet the neighbor that the Holy Spirit has been placing in your thoughts? While all these define a small measure of personal effort or giving, I would hardly classify any as a true sacrifice even close to the magnitude identified in either of the previous eras.

Or perhaps, sacrifice isn't even part of the equation anymore. Jesus was, after all, the One and only perfect sacrifice, the Lamb of God. He fulfilled all the requirements for all blood sacrifices and guilt offerings. We don't earn forgiveness with sacrifices any longer. Nor do we earn love points or any sort of special status or position with offerings.

There is a clear principle of giving laid out by Jesus; however, that goes far beyond just the simple sacrifices of the Old Testament. This is a giving that reflects an attitude of humility (it's more blessed to give than receive from Acts 20:35) and selflessness (that a man would lay his life down for a friend). It's reflected in giving out whatever we have (heal the sick, raise the dead, cleanse those who have leprosy, drive out demons. Freely you have received; freely give from

Luke 6:38). Give out of whatever gift you have received (Romans 12:6–8). As we see portrayed in the young church of Acts, there is a level of giving that foregoes personal wealth, personal comforts, personal gain. It's being willing to be martyred, tortured, denied personal position or power. Men are called to love their wives as Christ loved the church, giving Himself up for her to make her holy. Husbands are called to feed and care for their wives as he would his own body (Ephesians 5). There is in that type of picture a note of deep continual sacrifice—a message of constant, daily attention given to the needs of those entrusted to our care, a sacrifice of commitment to the well-being and care of another. It is not a type of sacrifice that earns anything, but one than is born out of a pure love motivation that *desires* to give of oneself.

This type of sacrifice today is uncommon. It is seen in only a small percentage of families, is even less prominent in the church, and is notably rare in our twenty-first-century society. I need to tell you, though, that it is not extinct. This sacrificial love that knew the pain of laying life down for another was evident in my early years, long before I ever understood the meaning of Jesus's sacrifice. It certainly was before I knew of a heavenly Father's love that would give so freely of Himself for me. Yet that is exactly the message I have come to know as I reflect on my own natural father's life.

Dad was an ordinary man in most ways. He was a star football player in high school in the early 1940s. He knew the pain of sacrificing time, money, and working out ways to play without offending his own dad who thought he was wasting his time. He learned to pursue his dream without the support or approval of his parents. He gave up much to follow his heart. He developed the dream of becoming a football coach and knew it would again cost him much in terms of work, time, money, and would again sacrifice the approval of his own dad. As he began his college football career, World War II broke out. Though by rights, attending college on a football scholarship, he could have waited, he immediately enlisted in the US Navy to serve his country. He was willing to put his personal dream on hold to give all he had to give—himself. Few realized at the time the extent of service that would be required of them, certainly not my dad; nevertheless, he continued to give of himself. It was a difficult time of life, at best, which he rarely spoke of in my growing-up years. He was separated for two solid years from his sweetheart (my mom) as well as all family while he sailed the South Pacific seas as a radar man taking four-hour shifts on and four hours off, around the clock, seven days a week for months at a time. He gave for his world, for his country, for his friends and family at home, for his future wife. I don't really know what kept him and others like him sane in those endless days of sacrifice and hardship. I wish I'd thought to ask him, but I never did. I never realized the depth of his selflessness until too late. But I see it now.

The next phase of his love offering to my mom happened as he returned home after years in the war at sea. Instead of asking her to sacrifice a home and family for a while longer so he could complete his college and pursue his dream, he accepted the offer from his new father-in-law and uncle-in-law to build them a little starter home close by. The catch was he had to settle for whatever jobs he could find (which were scarce due to all the men returning home) and sacrifice the dream. For the love of his bride, he laid down his personal dream and accepted the home for her. The children were already coming quickly. Another larger home was soon needed. Dad pursued other jobs, working to provide for his rapidly growing family in whatever ways he could. First one move. Then another. Then another. Always pushing for a better life for those who were dependent on him. Dad eventually settled in a career at a uniform and industrial rental place. I never knew him to speak of loving his work. He actually spoke of it very little. As an adult, I noted how my dad persevered and endured for years that which brought him little to no joy or personal satisfaction. His only hope was that, if he stayed just long enough, it would provide a means of income in retirement years for his aging bride.

Though Dad didn't speak fondly of his job, I heard him go on and on with great passion and zeal regarding the latest football news. Truly, Dad had laid down his own love, his own desires for the good of the others in his life whom he loved. He was never willing to cause Mom or the children hardship while he pursued a personal goal or dream. It became apparent that his goal was transformed from some personal dream to one of providing joy, comfort, and security for others. And he drew satisfaction and joy from that himself more and more as the years passed. Truly he had laid down his life for us.

Today, it is not difficult for me to picture a selfless heavenly Father who gives of Himself joyfully to see His children prosper. This is the kind of message I received from watching my own dad throughout my life. He served us with his life in just about every way. I recall many power struggles or heated interchanges between my parents concerning various plans, purchases, and decisions. One of Dad's shortcomings was his common reaction to say "No, we can't do that" as his standard first response. However, I frequently remember him changing his position as the "discussions" would continue to develop. It was clear he had a stronger desire to keep peace and fulfill the desires of his family rather than his own. I didn't realize just how significant that was for most of my life.

In fact, there was a time I totally misunderstood this trait of keeping the peace as a weakness. While admittedly, it has some downfalls, I never realized the love it portrayed for us and his willingness to lay himself down for the rest of us. Though from the exterior it looked like weakness at times, it was Dad's giving heart at work that changed his "no" to "yes." Dad's own upbringing and family experiences caused him to see things through a paradigm of limitations and never having enough, but his heart was to give of himself always. I see how God put my mom in his life to move him along that path. The sad paradox is that the thing that Dad gave for us, his football dream, remained a wedge between Mom and Dad all their lives until just before the end. It wouldn't be an honest account if I said there were no hard feelings about the sacrifice. That's what separates the earthly experience from the heavenly Father, however. Our heavenly Father not only gave sacrificially, he also did so with joy as Jesus endured the cross for the joy set before Him. There were moments of joy in it for my dad, though. He would beam with pride in our happiness, our accomplishments, our moments of success, and especially in the gathering of his children, grandchildren, and great-grandchildren around him.

One of the aspects of Dad's willingness to sacrifice for us became an annoyance to my siblings and me as my parents moved late into their retirement on very restricted funds. Even when Dad had very little money, he would still want to pay for things for us. I am convinced that he would have spent his very last dollar on us rather than his own personal needs. I used to be so frustrated by his insistent bickering over picking up the bill, but it's just another aspect of that sacrificial giving that knew no reason—only love.

It makes no sense to me as to why Father God would give the way He does. He gives when I don't know He's giving. He gives when I feel like I should do it on my own. He gives when I haven't earned it and when I don't feel like I deserve it. He's just always giving. He gives His forgiveness, His mercy, His grace, His authority, His life, and an endless list of things that cost Him great sacrifice to give—and still He gives. He gives when He's misunderstood and when He's taken for granted. He gives when He's taken advantage of and when the price is high. His desire is that we would prosper and experience as much of Him as possible so He continues to give. Though my earthly dad was not perfect always in his motives or ways of sacrificial giving, his message of sacrificing his life for the good of others was clear. And the joy he received at seeing his offspring prosper in even the smallest ways made it easy to understand the joy our heavenly Father receives from the gifts He gives us. The book of James tells us that every good and perfect gift is from the Father. I believe it with all my heart.

The stage was set for me to understand the concept of sacrificial giving as "good" from my childhood. Grasp it. Know its truth—the truth that it's an honor, a privilege, a joy unsurpassed by any other to lay your life down for another. Dad showed me how. I did it for my own family, and I am fulfilled. Dad's life was full and fulfilling through his gift of himself to others. His last days on earth were proof. The offspring of three generations gathered themselves to him from all across the country to show honor, respect and love to the one who never stopped giving. Though in terms of dollars, titles, and public honors he could have earned, the price of the sacrifice was far too high seemingly, the rich inheritance of love and relationships he left were priceless, to become a large investment in the generations yet to come.

I see the unmistakable parallel to our Savior. The Father's gift cost fame, fortune, and political influence, yet it became the investment which bought the future of all mankind. This lifestyle of laying a life down for others is one of the kingdom of heaven. It is my Father in heaven living and dying here on earth.

6

Provider and Protector

"We can't afford that!"

"Money doesn't grow on trees!"

These were common phrases I knew well because I heard them all too often growing up. That and similar verbiage were almost always the first responses to come out of my dad's mouth when there was a need or request outside of the purchases regularly made for basic needs. Dad would be blessed and honored probably now to know that I'm writing about what a good provider he was because this was probably the area of his greatest personal insecurities. I believe he even experienced guilt and regrets in the financial realm of his life. I heard him mention many times of how if only he had finished college, he'd be like some of his peers who had provided for their children's college educations, took nice vacations, and had comfortable retirement funds. These peers supposedly didn't experience the same pressure and burdens of his life because they finished college, were able to climb corporate ladders, or grow profitable businesses and received compensations for their worth. Occasionally, Dad would begin wandering down the path of recounting the things that he *couldn't* do and listing his limitations, all because of the choices he had made early on in his young adult life. His anxiousness to provide at that point actually cut short his long-term potential. At least that's how I always used to look at it—from human, materialistic eyes. This ungodly perspective coupled with my own judgments almost cost me the ability to see the true character of God that was modeled in my family as Dad provided for his large family.

There is another perspective. It is another higher way that focuses the vanishing point in the canvas of life in a completely different position on the horizon of our life portrait. With this transformed perspective, successes and failures have different hues and tones from those that many of us grew up painting ourselves with. Viewing life from the vantage point of the kingdom of God produces a completely different pallet of value colors. Our culture defines success so differently than our heavenly Father does. As my dad looked at his seemingly poor educational and financial decisions, he considered himself at the bottom of the heap. Yet late in life, he began to fully appreciate the riches he had attained in the relationships he had built with his family and with his God. Late in life, he would periodically mention some of those same "successful" peers that he would have previously envied. He talked about their plight of experiencing rejection or minimal tolerance from their children and grandchildren or the loneliness of an alienated spouse, feuding family members, or their lack of friendships with sadness and pity. He would sometimes mention his observation in his last years, how those with fat bank accounts and heavy investments bore heavy burdens of all different kinds related directly to the financial success they had attained. He noted that wealth does not equal peace, ease, or tranquility in life.

It was not until Dad was on his death bed, however, that I fully realized the extent of wealth my near-penniless father had accumulated. With a family of seven children and his one and only wife of his youth by his side, there came a multitude of grandchildren and great-grandchildren—a priceless fortune.

The image is seared in my memory even now, over a decade later, of Dad laying in his bed in what had been their sitting room. There was a door to the hallway on one wall. On the other side of the room were large sliding glass doors that opened to a beautiful pool nestled in a lush, tropical wraparound patio and yard. Through the hallway door, one by one, the family came. Over the previous several days, all had assembled from all over the country—children, grandchildren, great-grandchildren. There were at least forty of us. Dad had been expected to pass any day, but he had lingered day after day, hour after hour, much to my mom's dismay. She wanted him released from pain, from misery, from waiting. He was patient, though. Now, by some holy, unspoken beckoning, we were all there, altogether, passing by his bedside one-by-one, in this sacred procession. Each one entered into the room, paused beside him long enough to receive recognition and a blessing from Dad and then exited onto the patio by the pool into a solemn assembly. In this one impromptu act, Dad provided the most valuable, most precious gift a man can ever bestow on his family—his blessing.

In the Bible, in the last days of life, we see Abraham giving his blessing to Isaac, Isaac giving his blessing to Jacob and Esau, Israel (Jacob) blessing his twelve sons and the sons of Joseph. It is of highest value among the Jewish people, God's original chosen people. It is something that has been lost in the majority of our modern culture, but the value remains. I hear story after story of people with massive holes in their hearts because they never received their father's blessing. Many books have been written on the subject. Countless people suffer from the emptiness resulting from the absent or negligent patriarch that never took this role seriously and deprived their offspring of such a richness that can't be earned.

My dad hadn't read any books or listened to any messages that spoke of this, at least not that I am aware of. Yet he knew that before he died, it was one golden nugget he could deposit into each of us. I believe his words were simple for each of us. It wasn't traditional or long-winded. It was three words: "God love you." He wasn't a man that could easily say "I love you," yet we all experienced his love without question. Those three words blessed us with the love of God, which was clearly Dad's as well. I believe that our heavenly Father knew this was Dad's desire so He supernaturally called us from all over and made a way for every single one to come. He allowed my dad to tarry until all had arrived. Our Father in heaven desired to bless us all through our natural father with God's divine love. It is the greatest gift one can receive or give.

> If I have the gift of prophesy and can fathom all mysteries and all knowledge, and if I have faith that can move mountains, but have not love, I am nothing. If I give all I possess to the poor and surrender my body to the flames, but have not love, I gain nothing... And now these three remain: faith, hope and love. But the greatest of these is love. (1 Corinthians 13:2–3 and 13)

In the midst of my dad's fears and disappointments regarding his provisions over our lives, he found that which was of highest value. He found that which never loses its worth. It is valued throughout every generation for all time. He left it for each of us to be enriched by for the rest of our lives and to pass on to the generations following. He blessed us to be a blessing within our hurting world. It was so simple yet so profound.

This is how our heavenly Father provides for us. The parallel is unmistakable. While many have interpreted God's provisions in terms of dollars or material net worth, the greatest value of His provisions come in terms of the intangible. Love tops the list, but there are many others. They are packaged in the form of wisdom, fulfilling relationships, strength of character, sustaining faith, perseverance, joy, peace, undying hope, security that comes from our identity as His child and heir. I could continue with more, but you understand what I am saying. While I have never been particularly focused on material possessions, this demonstration of the inheritance I received from my dad in the form of his blessing and love has solidified this understanding in my heart. It has caused me to feel very rich indeed and blessed beyond many of my peers who sport beautiful homes, cabins, cars, boats, vacations, the latest greatest technology, and whatever they desire. There is no envy or jealousy or even desire for those things. I am blessed beyond my greatest imagination because of the inheritance of my dad's love and the family he left me.

There was more evidence of the way our heavenly Father provides in my dad's last days. It didn't stop with the richness of this revelation. In April, when he had that massive stroke, we all thought that was it. It wasn't. He lived seven more months. There were many days when I thought the Lord should take him now. That would be God's mercy. God didn't, though. My timing wasn't God's.

At that time, my parents lived in their own home just a few miles away from one of my sisters and her husband in southern Florida. The rest of us were many hundreds of miles away. As Dad struggled following his stroke, my sister and her husband decided to take our parents into their own home. They searched and found a place that would accommodate my parents in a way that they could remain somewhat independent but would be under their safe covering. It took months for that process to materialize. There were many hurdles to overcome, including the sale of my parents' home at a time when home values and sales were declining. Dad rallied through these days, up and down. Finally, the first weekend in November, things came together after scaling many hurdles. I flew from Minnesota to Florida to watch over my dad while the big move happened. It was a great comfort to know that my parents were now secured in a safe place, though we were all keenly aware of the challenge it would be for my sister and brother-in-law. The house seemed like a perfect setup, however, enabling both couples sufficient privacy with shared space when they wanted. It even had that beautiful pool that both couples had private access to. This enabled my parents to maintain their routine of regular swimming for exercise. It really couldn't have been more perfect. In spite of struggling emotionally with leaving my dad again in his weakened, vulnerable state, I left Florida feeling that they were securely tucked in for the long haul. It was good.

Within a few short days, however, the final decline began. It started suddenly and appeared to be progressing quickly as my dad was hospitalized once more then sent home with hospice care. He was now preparing to die. I don't think they had even been in the house two weeks! I was in shock. I thought this move would mean more time. It didn't. The real purpose that the Lord disclosed later was that our heavenly Father was making sure that my mom would be taken care of properly after my dad was gone. Who knew? My dad didn't die until he knew Mom was covered, cared for, and not alone in the house. This would have been my dad's desire, but it was fully Father God's doing. It hadn't transpired seamlessly, without problems. It carried a heavy price tag for my sister and brother-in-law who made the sacrifice. That's how it is sometimes, though. God makes provision, often moving through those who are willing to walk with Him to shoulder the natural side of the burden on earth. God did it for my mom, and He did it for my family. He undergirded my mom to steady her so that she wouldn't slip and fall spiritually or emotionally in a very vulnerable time of her life.

Jesus told us that He would not leave us or forsake us. The characteristics of Jesus are the same as our Father in heaven. Jesus told His disciples the night He was arrested just before His crucifixion, that when we see Him, we see the Father. They are the same, in perfect unity. Jesus told His disciples that when He left to go back to His He Father, He would send another, His Holy Spirit, the Comforter or Counselor, to be with us forever. Father God demonstrated this in a natural way for my mom. As my dad prepared to leave the earth, He provided others for my mom to care for her, comfort her, and be near. While I am fully aware that this is not always true in a natural sense for many people, Father God made a strong point of demonstrating that part of His character to me with this experience in my family. It is not in His nature or heart to leave us alone.

In the days that followed my dad's passing into eternity, I know my mom often felt lonely. Her soul mate and best friend of over sixty years was no longer physically present or visible. Yet she wasn't alone. There were two others in the house committed to her care and comfort. Often, we may feel alone, like God has abandoned us, but He hasn't. Not ever. His covering remains over our lives. He watches over our coming and going. Though we may feel like we're slipping, He never slumbers and keeps a fully attentive watch so that we don't fall beyond His reach. There is no sadness, no grief, no hardship, no dark pit that is beyond His grasp. Where our faith and our hope may shake and teeter in the storms of life, His great love remains always. It never fails.

You may say, "Yes, for those who are strong and devoted in their faith," but our Father God did not make that distinction. He said, "What mother can forget the child that nursed at her breast? So it is with you." Time after time, when His beloved chosen nation, Israel, was rebellious and faithless, Father God would reach down and draw them back into His protective covering. While it's true that we often bear the consequences of our own mistakes or rebellion, He always welcomes us into His presence when we turn to Him. He remains our provision and protection throughout the generations.

Each one of my dad's seven children had days of rebellion or turning away from him in some way. It didn't quench my dad's love for us, however. It didn't nullify his final blessing as we all turned to him. So it was on earth with my unknowing earthly dad, and so much more it is with our heavenly Father. We are told that if our father on earth knows how to give us good gifts, how much more does our good Father in heaven? He is desiring to bless you with His goodness, His love, His protection, His Holy Spirit. We only need to show up before Him to receive it. Father God has a rich inheritance for us all. It is Himself in all His fullness, His blessing, His love. There is nothing greater than this.

7

Sweeter Than Honey

Perhaps you've heard the analogy before of the Lord being "sweet." This is a concept that had always perplexed me. My heavenly Father, who is the God of all gods, Creator of the universe and beyond, Supreme, Almighty, Powerful One, Omniscient, Holy, Sovereign, Judge, King of kings—these are but a few of the many names defining the character of God that readily come to mind as I've grown to know my God more personally over the span of my life. But sweet? Honestly, though I'd heard the term in reference to our God, sung of it, and read about it, it never entered my thoughts at the beginning of my meditations on the Lord, at the end, nor anywhere in between. I simply had no "father" reference point relating to sweet. It certainly wasn't a masculine term in my encyclopedia of experience. Perhaps in considering the fruit of the Holy Spirit and encountering kindness, gentleness, or meekness, one could begin to enter a similar arena as sweetness, but not really.

After all what *is* sweet? Babies are sweet. Girls and even some grown women can be sweet. Young boys can be sweet, but the trait is lost the closer to manhood a boy grows. It implies a certain innocence portioned with huge doses of kindness and gentleness. It demands a look of acceptance or even adoration toward the recipients of sweetness. It encompasses a tone that soothes, comforts, and invites one into the eyes and heart of the sweet. It trusts with almost an air of naiveté. Its flavor is delicious, stirring the desire for more and is pleasing to body and mind alike.

Nothing could be farther from my he-man Provider, Protector God who thunders billowing smoke and fire from Mt. Zion. He is my God who calms the seas with overpowering authority and sends powerful demons to flight, trembling with fear. He is without question good and right in all His judgments and actions…but sweet?

So what did the psalmist perceive when he penned the verses testifying that the words of the Lord were sweeter than honey in his mouth (Psalm 119:103) and God's judgments were sweeter than honey from the honeycomb (Psalm 19:10)? What could the present-day songwriter possibly mean when he sang that His "name is like honey on my lips"? To be honest, I had never given it much thought. To say that I puzzled over it without arriving at any viable conclusion would be completely untrue. It meant so little to me that I never even thought to ponder it!

I never considered it, that is, until the day that I witnessed the transformation of my own dad here on earth. His transformation came through much pain. It was a physical pain for certain as he challenged his body to renew lost strength and coordination. Much more, however, was the mental and emotional pain of the provider becoming the provided for, the giver becoming the recipient, the strong humbled to simple frailty, reliant on the strength of those previously far inferior to his strength. In the midst of his return to a dependent state (*return*, I note, because do we not all begin life completely dependent in our infant, childlike state?), a new nature, foreign to me, began to emerge. His childlike perspectives emerged with a very definite new flavor or savor if you will, which I began to recognize as undeniable sweetness. Sweetness as an aura about him. Sweetness oozing through his words. Sweetness radiating from his face. Sweetness encompassing his touch. I had considered my dad with much admiration, to be many things. He was good, strong, protective, wise, and always helpful, an encourager, kind, sometimes even gentle. Sweet, however, would have been quite possibly last or more likely nonexistent on any list of positive traits I would have used to describe my dad. Here it was, though, unmistakably in the forefront of all of my interactions with him in his weakened state.

This began my quest to search out how this could be. Was he faking it to sweeten up his caregivers? No, there was not even a hint of manipulation or bribery in his demeanor. His emotions and responses were candid, real, unguarded as never before. That was not it. I observed repeatedly this unusually perplexing mix of masculine sweetness. It began to add warmth from the inner parts of my soul to my outer extremities. At the same time, it stirred such a delightful attraction within me as to cause me to want to stick right by my dad's side and not leave.

This was a completely new experience. As a child, I had a difficult time making decisions that would separate me from the safe presence of my parents. I would regularly battle that sick feeling in the pit of my stomach with even the thought of spending the night away from home without them. From the time I reached my own young adulthood at the ripe old age of eighteen, however, I ran off to my new life in college, hours away from home and never looked back. I had outgrown that childlike adhesive to my parents. There was no sweetness to draw me back and no sticky goo of the honeylike substance to hold me there. I was independent, confident that I could do anything I set my mind to. My sights were set on being separate from my parents—from their business, their home, their lifestyle, their church. Now I found myself being irresistibly drawn back to my dad by this sweet demeanor that had overtaken him. It was as an obsession can be. When I was away from him, thoughts of him were ever present, mixed with the desire to be there with him just a little longer, a little more. No matter how much time I'd spent, it was never enough.

In puzzlement over my "sweet" dad, as I sat one night marveling over how wonderful it was to be with him, my heavenly Dad began to speak to me. "This," He spoke to my heart, with inaudible words, "is what the sweetness of the Lord is like. You have missed an entirely wonderful aspect of My character simply because it was out of your sphere of reference. Allow Me to show you now."

This began an amazing quest for me as I began to discover how rich the sweetness of the Lord is. Truly, the name of Jesus is sweeter than honey on my lips. There is no sweeter name than the name of Father. I began to understand how it's that irresistible gooey kindness that brings us to repentance. If repentance is the turning away from one way of life and moving into the complete opposite direction, then it was the sweetness that caused me to no longer want to be away from my Father but only want to be near Him. I wanted to be with my Lord always, knowing that He had that same quality of acceptance, encouragement, unconditional love, sincere appreciation that He desired to pour out on me with every encounter. I realized that it was not our heavenly Father's way for us to move away from Him in independence, never looking back. It was His way to keep us glued to Himself, always desiring to be with Him, luring us there with His incredible sweetness.

Perhaps Father God had always approached me in such a way, but I wasn't able to see it. I was steeped in my independence and self-sufficiency. What I witnessed in my dad, however, revealed a rather painful truth. My dad's position of need and even my own state of vulnerability in the emotional and spiritual upheaval I was experiencing while witnessing the decline of my dad hinted that sweetness and humility were somehow interrelated. There is a sweet savor that is spilled out when selfish pride is shattered and falls off in the midst of a life being broken. It is the fragrance others enjoy when the shattered soul is lifted to our God humbly, without blame or anger, but with dedication and resolve to be whatever He desires in that broken state. You see, there was very little if any, fist shaking at God from Dad. Instead, there had grown a tree planted by the stream of the Lord that, out of delight in the Lord and a seeking of His ways, continued to bear its fruit in season, just as Psalm 1 prophecies. As the temptation to fall into anger and bitterness over the condition of his last days was resisted, and my dad yielded to whatever the Lord desired for that day, one day at a time, a new sweet fruit, which very much resembled honey, came into season in my dad's life for the rest of us to enjoy and learn from.

In that place of broken humility, the most profound truth is found—the viewpoint of the extreme value of those around us. As we offer the nothing that we have become to our Father, His adoration of this completely dependent, near helpless child is perceived perhaps for the first time. We are drawn to Him through His irresistibly comforting warmth of welcoming acceptance, appreciation, encouraging love, otherwise known as sweetness. One cannot help but see the value of others and ooze with this same honey once they have been filled with it themselves through the humility and brokenness in their own lives.

Father God began to open up for the first time to me how His sweetness, as portrayed by my dad, could not only draw me to Him, but cause me to remain as Jesus instructed us to do in John 15:4. For those of us who come to know Him but then mistakenly run off to live an independent life with the riches we've been raised with, there is a message loud and clear. It is this—His kindness, His love, His adoration of you, His delight in you, His tender encouragement and comfort He gives are all meant to draw us and keep us close to Him. When we receive this part of His nature and character, we *want* to be near Him, just as He wants us to be. He prepares a place for us to remain with Him as His children.

Honey is known to be sweet nutrition. It's good for you and provides strength in a pleasing form. The tender words of affection and encouragement we receive through the Bible and sense from Him in our spirit are that honey. Many of us have difficulty receiving affirmation or love in various forms, but this is sweetness He provides to draw us near to Him, to remain with Him. The Song of Songs is filled to overflowing with affectionate, sweet love between Jesus and His bride, us, the church, yet many are unable to receive this kind of sweetness from Creator Father God. Just as I had no idea this character could or should be resident in my earthly dad, I had missed it as well in my heavenly Father. But this is who He is, and this is how He keeps us close! As a couple are drawn together for life by the sweet passionate love they receive and give between each other, so it is the glue that keeps us connected to our God in faithfulness, rather than running off to other lovers in independence. We long for and even become dependent on that sweetness that is poured out. It is where you run to when comfort, encouragement, strength are needed.

In the midst of my dad's last months on earth, I suffered a personal tragedy far surpassing anything I had previously known. My husband and I were pastoring our small congregation at the time, which had weathered some difficulties in the previous several months regarding a rapidly decreasing financial base, loss of our assistant pastor of five years, and loss of our worship director of eight years. We struggled through what we imagined to be the worst of it when the tragedy struck one of our close families. My husband and I had known this family since before the couple was married, and they now had five children, ages seventeen to four. They had weathered many storms, more challenging than average, and had developed a firm steadfastness in faith. The father displayed an uncommon gift of faith, in fact, and the mother was an anointed worshipper whose voice touched all those around her deeply as she filled the air with songs to her heavenly Father. Nothing prepared any of us for the devastation ahead, though.

On a beautiful October afternoon, just as we were preparing dinner, Jay, my husband, answered the phone to receive the message from one of our church leaders (a close friend of the father) that the father had accidently backed his vehicle over their youngest child on their property, and the child was dead. In shock and disbelief, Jay immediately called the family and spoke with a hysterical, frantic mother, whose undecipherable screams and sobs confirmed the report. The following hours will unfortunately be etched in my memory of horrors that I have wished a thousand times over to forget. The days and weeks ahead stretched all of us to places beyond ourselves we had never thought of going. I wish I could tell you that the child was raised from the dead. He was not. I wish I could tell you the family was somehow spared devastation. They were not. All I can say is that a miraculous work of a body of believers pulling together to share the burden of pain and grief happened, and God has been glorified as not one turned away from Him in anger or bitterness.

Instead, an entire community of people turned toward their Father and received the comfort and peace He wanted to give in the midst of a horrific storm. The sharing of the whole story is certainly another book with many chapters. I will share, however, that the first night, when Jay and I finally returned home late, leaving the family guarded by the company of close friends from the church, I needed desperately to be comforted myself. I tossed and turned in the night, though, exhausted. I paced and cried out to God in the night. I searched His word. I knelt before Him. I fell on my face, pleading before Him. The shock and depth of pain and despair I experienced personally and with the family had completely emptied me. I was certain God was with us, but I had no sense of what He wanted to speak or show or be to us then. There was a numbness that would not allow Him to penetrate. As the night became the light of morning, the void in me gradually turned to fear and confusion. I needed something to give this family. I needed the words to give those in our congregation who surely would be suffering shock and grief as I had been. If Jay and I had nothing to offer our people, then who? It was our heavy burden at that hour to shepherd a deeply wounded suffering flock. Neither of us had a clue of what to do, how to comfort under such circumstances.

It was under these conditions that I called my parents that morning after wrestling my way through the night. Hearing my mom and dad's voices brought great comfort. The sweet compassion in their voices were as nourishment to me. Dad actually had no great words of wisdom for this situation, but his and mom's tender words of encouragement and confidence in me gave me just enough to go on. More than the actual words was the tone with which they were spoken. I had tried to go directly to God but was too deep in shock to receive from Him. The Lord used His sweetness in Dad (and Mom) to draw me back to Him where I could receive directly once again, which I did repeatedly in the following days. This is the kind of God who fathers us so perfectly. He refuses to leave us without comfort, without hope. If we are willing to receive His words, He will never leave us without what we need for life and godliness (2 Peter 1:2). He refuses to leave us feeling forsaken and abandoned. He continues to reach across miles, years, and obstacles of all kinds to provide sweet nourishment through compassionate grace, mercy, love.

God humbled Himself and broke Himself by coming to earth in human form as Jesus and endured the cross. It was an act of love that spoke through generations to every soul ever known to mankind. It was His way to restore fellowship with us because He wants us with Him that much. Jesus pointed the way to our Father. He repeatedly acted in humility, moved out of compassion, and allowed any personal desires to be broken in perfect obedience to His Father's desire. He displayed the tender sweet mercies and love in His interactions with the worst of sinners, the smallest of children, and the boldest of His disciples. I challenge you to read the gospels anew. You will find a sweet-like-honey Jesus appear repeatedly, consistently—one who has tender words of affection, showing value and love for the individual.

Though I had previously missed the message of the sweetness of the Lord, out of His great love and mercy, He used my own father to reveal it to me at a time when I needed it more than ever before in my life. Is He trying to pour out tender words of affection on you, but you are missing it? Allow His words of love to flow over you as warm, flowing, thick honey. Allow it to strengthen and nourish you. Honey was listed as one of the prime, most desirable products of the land in many Old Testament accounts. His sweetness is most valuable in our lives. You must know that He is tender as with children. He is not rough, harsh, or angry. His gentleness soothes the pain of correction. His deep loving mercy and grace take the sting from sin and death as we receive forgiveness with repentant hearts as with Mary Magdalene or Matthew the tax collector. He says come to Him and receive rest. He soothes our anxious minds with an assurance that will leave us cloaked in peace that transcends understanding. He shows us sweet love that goes beyond the grave, His love that is everlasting, unconditional, and can never be taken from us. Receive it. Believe it. Allow it to penetrate you as never before, for it is deeper, wider, higher, longer than any one of us can comprehend. So dig into Him and let Him show you the deeper, higher, wider, longer aspect of His sweetness you've yet to grasp. It's life to you, strength, and causes you to never want to leave Him. It fills you with a desire to be with Him always, receiving from Him always, being a vessel through which His sweet love is continually dispensed to others as well.

This is our Father in heaven as He is with us now.

8

Our Father's Will on Earth

What do you think of when you think of doing God's will? What enters your mind as you consider God's will for your life? Perhaps it is wrapped in a blanket of fear, being afraid that His desires for you include tasks or places that you loathe. Perhaps considerations of His will are jammed inside the box that contain all the strict dos and don'ts, the *rules* compiled by "the church" or the Bible. Perhaps for you, God's will is entangled in the chains of obedience like some slave in bondage to fulfill the commands of his master. Maybe that elusive "will of God" is something dangling before you, just beyond reach, as some seemingly unattainable dream that drives you on to perform, but you never seem to quite hit the mark. Scripturally, you can find verses to support every one of these perspectives.

I have found myself in every one of these mindsets at one time or another in my journey with Jesus. Personally, following the Lord's call into foreign missions has been cloaked in various weights of fear throughout the years. I've had to push through all manner of fears to fulfill His will for my life on earth as it is in heaven. I remember when I first started feeling the nudge to personally involve myself in missions work outside of the US. It began with giving money to missionaries. That was easy. I wrote a check and put it in the basket. Then came a nagging sense to provide monthly support to a missionary in Spain. That was a little harder, but it was still pretty painless.

Then came sending Jay to Russia. That had a much greater price tag, attached by a string of various discomforts.

It wasn't the money because someone felt so strongly about Jay going, that the minute he expressed a desire, they provided the funds. The difficulty was my situation when he went. I was left at home with three young children, ages nine, six, and four, while battling a serious draining illness. Coughing up blood, I found out the day he left that I had pneumonia. Mustering up my courage and faith, I insisted he still go in spite of my condition. Already, this trip had been postponed once due to political situations beyond our control. This time, we both felt even more strongly that he needed to go. After he left, in my much-weakened state, I had convinced myself that Jay was going to be detained or worse, die, and he wasn't coming back. This was in the days prior to easy access to internet communications or Wi-Fi technology, so there were no phone calls, no messages, no communication at all for his entire time away. In fact, at one point, Jay had been under the impression he would be able to make a call home only to find the cord between the phone receiver and the phone base completely cut through and not even attached!

I was driven to almost continuous prayer for long hours as I laid without strength, moving from the bed to the couch, the couch to bed restlessly. The prayer was a good thing, though. There were some amazing things that resulted in that prayer time from my sick bed. I tried to listen to the Holy Spirit, and as I followed Him in intercession, the fear would lift. I would feel connected to Jay and his team, and I would sense good things, *exciting* things happening. Today, with as difficult as it was then, I would definitely make the same choice again if it was presented. It was the beginnings of a foundation for much to come as God would lead us in the future into our destiny of expanding His kingdom in the nations. It was a trial that matured us just a little bit more, strengthened our faith just a little bit more, taught us to trust God's ways, timing and love just a little more. You see, growth in the spiritual child happens much as it happens in the body of a natural child. You don't see it happen before your eyes, but it's in the hidden moments that it happens, minuscule bit by minuscule bit until an inch, one small inch becomes evident by the way the clothes fit or how the stature measures next to another familiar figure or place. This first trip was like the birth of what was conceived and growing in the previous years of missions giving. The missions baby had finally grown enough to enter the world. It was a painful birth and rude awakening into the new world, but it was God's good and perfect will.

The next summer came an opportunity for me to go to Mexico. While I sensed a prompting to go, I didn't pray or ask God about it because that same fear settled in me again only to a greater degree. I didn't ask God about going because I was afraid He would say, "Yes, go!" Just a couple of weeks before the team's scheduled departure, however, I broke down and talked to God about it. My love for Him won over the fear. I agreed to go. I thought I was going so I could be some great blessing to the people in Mexico, but in reality, it was training ground for me. More inch-by-tiny-inch growth. It was the first of many lessons to come in humility and serving those around me in love, no matter who they are, how they act, or how they smell. The greatest challenge on this trip was myself and my critical attitude toward others on the team who didn't serve the way I thought they should. I entered the School of Humility and Unconditional Love. This course would prove to present extremely challenging curriculum in the years to come. It was a major reason why I battled fear again, much later in life, when wrestling against following God's will for Jay and me to fully devote ourselves to missions work. If I had understood my Father's great love for me and the joy He has in having me partner with Him in what He is doing, it would have been much easier. I had to learn these lessons of His love and joy the hard way, though, until I was able to understand that there is always peace in His will. He is, after all, the Prince of Peace! Even so, from our human perspective, it can feel unsettling and scary to walk in His will for a multitude of reasons.

For instance, there's muddling through the legalistic requirements of following God's rules perfectly in order to be in His will. While "the rules" may appear simple and clearly defined, understanding how to apply them personally can be as difficult as comprehending the contents of volumes of complicated law books! Due to my background of substance abuse, including heavy marijuana use, experimentation with street drugs along with lots and lots of alcohol, I became very judgmental and legalistic concerning all alcohol use, even for communion. I became rigid in my approach to other Christians who held more relaxed views of alcohol use. While clearly drunkenness is inappropriate for a follower of Jesus, for myself, I felt that even a sip of wine was unacceptable or out of God's will for my life. I had bought into the philosophy that once an alcoholic, always an alcoholic, and even a glass of wine at dinner or a sip of a wedding champagne toast could throw me back into an alcoholic binge. And I judged others with the same measuring stick. It wasn't until I began to interact with European pastors that I realized there is freedom in different cultures to have a glass of wine or beer without any temptation for drunkenness. Why was it different in my circle of believers in the US? For many years, I had thought that God's will meant a zero tolerance for any form of alcohol in the life of a believer for any reason. During those years, that was holiness to me. Complete abstention from alcohol was God's perfect and pleasing will. But was it really? Where did that leave my newfound European pastor friends who were clearly very anointed, lovers of God, doing great things in His kingdom with much good fruit to show for it in their personal lives and ministries? Were they *unholy*? Were they sinners? Apparently, our Father in heaven still liked hanging out with them! What was *really* the Father's will concerning this matter?

This brings me to the question then of how Jesus settled these issues in life. He certainly encountered and confronted many controversial situations that the authorities of the time considered cut and dried. What is the perspective of Jesus when He tells us to pray for our Father's will to be done on earth as it is in heaven? "Your kingdom come, Your will be done on earth as it is in heaven" (Matthew 6:10). I believe that there is a higher, deeper, more perfect way to walk in our Father's will. It became evident to me in a fresh new light when I was spending time with my dad that last July (about four months) before he died. He was in such a weakened state that he needed assistance throughout much of his day. Eating, using the bathroom, and moving about the house were about the extent of his independence. Superficially, he could communicate well, but his memory and comprehension were greatly impaired. Reading and writing were practically impossible, though he tried. His days were filled with frustration, disappointment, and sometimes tears as he felt the constraining burden of his limitations. Always, though, he was thankful. He was appreciative of the companionship and help from those around him, in spite of the humiliation he felt in his needy state. His appreciation for each new day ran deep as he would awaken each morning and cheerfully announce as he got out of bed (with no small effort), "Well, the Good Lord must have something for me to do today because I'm still here!"

The first time I witnessed this, it shocked me. I knew what his days were like. I knew his abilities were less than a shrunken shadow of what he used to do. Yet here he is, even with a cheerful demeanor, approaching this new day with a heart that expected to have purpose. He expected to seek out and find the reason for his breath that day. He expected that no matter how much he couldn't do, the Lord had a desire for something that he *could* do or be. In that, his life still had value, purpose, worth. Because he was still breathing, he figured the Lord would use that breath for His will that day, regardless of what Dad could or could not do.

Wow! What a revelation this brought to my heart concerning my perspective on God's will. Every day carries purpose, opportunity, something of value to our Father. Approaching each day with a perspective of "What's on Your mind today, Father? I know You have something in mind because I'm still breathing here on earth!" is so refreshing! I am strengthened and encouraged because I know that today, I matter. What I do matters because *I* matter to Him. The people around me matter to Him. He has something on His heart for me for this day. There's a reason I am here today. It might be something small like showing love and appreciation with a smile, a pat on the hand, a thank-you to someone around you in a way that leaves that person feeling encouraged, valued, and loved, like my dad did almost daily. There were those of us that needed that, especially my mom.

It might be those simple interactions that bring healing to a wounded relationship with an apology, a tear, a kind word of appreciation, again like happened between my parents. Those healing interactions were critical to my mom's purpose in continuing on after Dad's death. It might be something big, like revealing God in an amazing new light, which has a life changing impact on how you love, teach, and present God in general as you go out into all the world, as it did with me. In the most humble of circumstances, one common individual can have a worldwide impact with the simple attitude of looking to fulfill God's desire for that day. It need not be an intense seeking, burdensome searching, or a debilitating time of waiting until you know "the plan." I realized that doing God's will daily can be as simple as maintaining that cheerful mindset of "Okay, Lord! I know You have something for me today. I'm all Yours, so lead me through the day according to how You see it!" Our Father's kingdom coming to earth is a matter of bringing righteousness, peace, and joy through the Holy Spirit to those around us. "For the kingdom of God is not a matter of eating and drinking, but of righteousness, peace and joy in the Holy Spirit, because anyone who serves Christ in this way is pleasing to God and approved by men" (Romans 14:17–18).

It doesn't need to be complicated or difficult or intense or frightening or costly. Although there are times it may seem like that, most of the time, I mean on a regular, mundane, everyday basis, His will being done on earth as it is in heaven is simple. It's a matter of acting in God's likeness, which is love. What does it act like or look like? It looks like righteousness, joy, and peace, as played out according to the great love chapter in 1 Corinthians 13. Patience, kindness, being polite, and humility are all big on God's list for your day. It's His way for you. It's His will and it is how you can bring His kingdom to earth! It's so simple that even an eighty-four-year-old man with little strength and few capabilities can hit the mark dead center every day, having a worldwide impact through those that he touches right from his own home.

Of course, there's the big stuff that requires big faith and big prayers to discern and walk out His will. However, a much greater portion of our life is defined by the daily little stuff like sharing a little kindness or joy or putting someone else first or forgiving. Righteousness, joy, and peace. A lot of simple gestures and attitudes fit under these three umbrellas and cast a shadow of heaven onto the earth. In my dad's weakness, I learned that God's will on earth was far simpler and far more important than I ever had imagined. Love. Thanksgiving. Honor. All at the top of God's daily agenda. As the days wane into years, they remain critical components in any long-term path the Lord has laid out for us.

Our Father's will on earth, I am convinced, encompasses daily submission to seeking out and yielding to righteousness, peace, and joy by following the Holy Spirit. In choosing this as a lifestyle, He will lead us into the big stuff naturally (or maybe I should say *super-naturally*). Then, when the direction is felt or sensed (like feeling I should go to Mexico but didn't want to ask!), we can enter into that place of talking to our heavenly Father about it, and He will lead. He will give the direction we need when we need it. He'll make the necessary provisions at the right times. He'll give the courage, strength, and help. It begins with the daily simple steps, though. *"Well, the good Lord must have something for me to do today because I'm still here!"*

Are you ready for the fulfillment of the simple prayer, "Let Your will be done on earth as it is in heaven," to be fulfilled in your daily life? It's as easy as submitting your life to the direction of the Holy Spirit. Recognize that the way of our Father in heaven is good. Trust that His plans for your life and each day is good. He assures us of His good plans and that He wants us to discover them. "'For I know the plans I have for you,' declares the Lord, 'plans to prosper you and not to harm you, plans to give you hope and a future. Then you will call on me and come and pray to me, and I will listen to you. You will seek me and find me when you seek me with all your heart'" (Jeremiah 29:11–13). James 1:17 says, "Every good and perfect gift is from above, coming down from the Father of the heavenly lights, who does not change like shifting shadows." His goodness is declared throughout the book Psalms repeatedly. There is no need to fear His perfect will because it is good!

Finally, set your mind on the things of the Spirit. Let Him lead you daily, like my dad in his restricted, humble last days. If we have our minds set on carnal, temporal things, our lives take on the stench of sin and death. If we set our minds on the eternal things like relationships in the context of peace, joy, and righteousness, all from the foundation of love, our lives are life-giving, bearing eternal fruit. According to Romans 8:5–6, "Those who live according to the flesh have their minds set on what the flesh desires; but those who live in accordance with the Spirit have their minds set on what the Spirit desires. The mind governed by the flesh is death, but the mind governed by the Spirit is life and peace." It requires a mind shift where we are changed from being shaped by the world to being shaped by the Spirit. In this frame of mind, we are able to discern God's perfect will, great and small. Romans 12:2 affirms this with the exhortation, "Do not conform to the pattern of this world, but be transformed by the renewing of your mind. Then you will be able to test and approve what God's will is—his good, pleasing and perfect will." God wants to be found and what He wants you to find is really good and attainable! Dad impacted a worldwide ministry from his humble little living room in the midst of some of his greatest weaknesses with his mind set on the simple purpose for the day—to do what God had for this day. If he could do that, just imagine what you can do.

9

Dad's Hands

As I sit in reflection of my life with my dad, his hands stand out to me. Dad had strong, handsome, even if you will, beautiful hands. As a plant supervisor, his hands weren't marred, calloused, or scarred as one who labors hard with their hands to earn a living. His fingers were long and lean, tipped with well-groomed nails. He had clean hands and didn't like getting them too dirty. I recall that he didn't enjoy eating crunchy tacos in particular because they were too messy! He really was uncomfortable with messy hands. In fact, in general, he didn't like messes.

One might think that such beautiful hands lacked strength. This was not so. Dad had been an athlete, a football player specifically, in his younger years. He wrestled playfully with young children, and often lifted them into his lap or to carry them in his arms. As years progressed, he took on tasks, which became hobbies, of remodeling and carpentry work to provide for the ever-changing needs of his expanding family. He performed a multitude of interior and exterior home projects. He also gardened for a period of time. Late in his life, he used wood chisels with expertise to create especially meaningful and fun wood carvings for the family. Even in the use of his hands, however, he never neglected their care, always cleaned and restored to their well-groomed state. His activities ensured that he maintained strong hands. They were the extended expression of the strength my dad carried in his physical body. I never doubted his strength.

In his strength, though, he was never rough or harsh with me. I can't say for sure if that was true with my older siblings, but as my dad grew in his life as a father, I have been told that he became gentler, more lenient, more controlled. Honestly, as any parent with multiple children knows, he probably grew wiser as to what was important, as well as a bit more tired with each one in a way that can translate into gentler, kinder ways. As the sixth of seven children, that was the dad that I knew—strength held in check. Our family wasn't big on hugs, unless you were saying goodbye for a long season, returning from the same or some special congratulations were in order. Dad's hands were all important, though, because with his frequent pats on my shoulder or on my hand he communicated his strength, love, acceptance, assurance, support, and even compassion. So much was communicated with his touch. It was one of his primary ways of expressing his love.

In his later years, in addition to a simple gold wedding band, he wore a beautiful garnet and gold ring on his right hand that had been a special gift. In spite of being a common man, his ring always made me think of him as being somewhat more regal or noble. He wore it well with confidence and a bit of pride. I know it was one of his few treasured material possessions.

Today, remembering Dad's hands brings revelation of parallels to our heavenly Father's hands. I am reminded of how often the Bible mentions the hand of God. First is the *mighty right hand of God.* While my own Dad was left-handed so his main strength was in his left hand, generally, the right hand is considered to be stronger. The vast majority of people are right-handed. So the mighty *right* hand of God speaks of Him providing His strength, His might through the touch or grasp of His hand. It speaks of God's ability to hold us, carry us, provide for us, protect us, cover us, guide us, lead us, and even bring us joy. Let's explore that together.

In Psalm 16, we see a reference to how God Himself is set at *our* right hand to bring strength, stability, and a place of security where we won't be shaken but can rest. It goes on then to say how out of that place where we are near to our God, He gives direction for our life. The result of being in this place near to Him is being filled with joy. It says, "I have set the Lord always before me. Because He is at my right hand, I will not be shaken" (verse 8). What does it mean to "set the Lord always before me?" It is a packed statement with many facets to consider. It is to put Him first in all things to begin with. He is my priority. Worship, prayer, learning His ways through scripture and sound biblical teaching are of utmost importance on a continual basis in my life. With the Lord always before me, I am watching Him carefully to follow His lead, looking for His direction and wisdom in every path of life. He is always first. He is in front of me, meaning, I am looking to see things through the filter of His ways, a godly perspective or view of the world, the people and situations that are around me. Since God's ways are higher than ours, and no one can fathom the depths of His knowledge and wisdom, I am always seeking to grow in knowing Him and His ways more and more. Having the Lord always before me means He is my priority, my guide, and I am looking to follow Him. In order to follow Him, I need to be able to discern His ways, His heart. That means that one of the highest priorities in my life is spending time doing things that help me get to know my Father so that I *can* discern His ways and His heart. He is considered first because He *is* first. In fact, He is *the* First (the Alpha) and *the* Last (the Omega).

This passage goes beyond the place of having the Lord before me, though. It continues with "Because He is at my right hand, I will not be shaken." Let's delve into that thought. We have already established the right hand as a symbol of our strength. What if we have someone *at* our right hand? It brings to mind the expression "He is my right-hand man," which basically implies that the person referred to is one who is close, relied upon for help or assistance, is trustworthy, and loyal. A "right-hand man" is someone you can count on. It is someone who will do things on your behalf that others may not be willing to do. He may carry your authority to complete transactions that others don't have the authority to do. It's a person you have full confidence in to remain with you through thick and thin. A right-hand man handles things for you and with you.

Now transfer this concept to having Jesus as your right-hand man. He has all power and authority beyond all others. His strength is beyond all others. His wisdom, patience, kindness, knowledge, goodness, and love are uniquely above and beyond all others. These things are what we have access to when "He is at my right hand." Amazing. Unfathomable. Yet He is always available to us when we set *Him* in place at our right hand, as our strength.

The results of having God at our right hand are revealed in Psalm 16 as well. We are told that it will prevent us from being "shaken." He provides stability as our rock. While we may feel shaky or unstable, He holds us and keeps us from falling. It was Jesus that walked on the water, invited Peter to join Him in the turbulent currents, and Jesus that reached out with His hands to keep Peter from going under. With Jesus as our right-hand man, relying on His strength or wisdom or whatever, we never need to fear drowning beneath the stormy waves of life. He is the rock that emerges when nothing else is in sight because He is always present through His Spirit, right there with us. Psalm 34 repeats this concept, saying, "Though he stumble, he will not fall, for the Lord upholds him with His hand." He brings security and causes us to rest in that security. Again, Psalm 139 repeats the theme with verse 5, "You have laid your hand upon me," and verse 10, "Your hand will guide me, your right hand will hold me fast." Security. Strength. Guidance. They are constant themes in reference to God's hands touching us in a very personal way, as individuals.

Another important benefit of keeping the Lord at your right hand is pleasure and joy. We live in a society that often seeks personal pleasure above other more important virtues. We have in our constitution that we have a right to pursue happiness. Yet few understand or accept the biblical truth of Psalm 16:11, that "You will fill me with joy in Your presence, with eternal pleasures at Your right hand," "You" and "Your" referring to God Himself. True joy, pleasure that never ends are found in that place of remaining close to our Father, allowing Him to hold us and guide us with His own right hand. Have you ever experienced the joy or pleasure of walking as a child, holding the hand of your parent? There's security, guidance, and strength there as well as the joy of being together, touching in a loving way. This is true with our heavenly Father. What about a romantic friendship where lovers walk side by side holding hands, enjoying the joy of a simple touch as a way of connection and closeness. While human relationships afford a measure of joy and pleasure, nothing compares to that which can be experienced in the presence of our God!

Another striking parallel in the remembrance of my dad's hands was his attention to keeping them clean and groomed. I don't know that he was aware of the specific scriptural reference to clean hands, but in his heart, I am sure he was devoted to staying clean before his God. This translated as well to his physical condition. Psalm 24 speaks of those who are qualified to ascend the hill of the Lord and stand in the holy place. It is those with clean hands and a pure heart. They are the ones who receive blessing and vindication from the Lord. They are ones who are known for seeking God's face and looking to Him for life.

Clean hands draw a strong spiritual connection to our ability to be close and stand before our Father since the beginning of the old covenant with Moses and the priests of that time. The first thing inside the door to the courtyards before entering the tabernacle which housed the presence of God was the altar to make sacrifices on for the forgiveness of sins (to purify the heart!). The next thing they would encounter was the laver or wash basin where they were required to wash their hands and feet before going any further. The washing occurred immediately following the sacrifice made at the altar. Ceremonial washing became an important part of the culture, spanning from requirements for washing before eating all the way to a mikvah or full bath for women following their monthly cycle or before their wedding. Washing was even part of Jesus's final acts with His disciples as He washed their feet at the last supper before He went to the cross.

Cleanliness of heart and hands is critical for those wanting to be as close as possible to God. You can be saved by grace through faith which is an amazing gift from our God as stated in Ephesians 2:8 by Paul, the infamous theologian and evangelist of the New Testament. We don't have to stop there, however. We're also invited into a closer, more intimate relationship with our Father through Jesus and His Holy Spirit. He calls us to be one with Him and to see His glory.

That happens as we are cleansed. Cleansing comes through forgiveness, both receiving it when we ask and granting it to others. It comes through repentance, which simply put, means behavior that changes as a result of a changed mind—thinking, perspectives, or attitudes that have been transformed from an old sinful viewpoint to one that reflects God's heart and ways. There is a deeper place of knowing Him beyond the salvation experience or just knowing the stories or words from the Bible at a surface level. There is a place of ascending the hill into His presence for those willing to be cleansed as often as He calls us to. The Holy of Holies, in the tabernacle of the old covenant, where the presence of God rested, was entered into only through sacrifice and cleansing. In the new covenant, Jesus provided the sacrifice and initial cleansing for entrance, but to rest in that inner place of His presence today, Jesus challenges us to cleanse our hearts through a lifestyle of continual forgiveness as I described previously.

It is an interesting side note that King David, who is known to be a man after God's heart, a man who was passionate, zealous, and quite demonstrative in his love for God, was not allowed to do the thing that was his life's desire. He wanted to build a house as a place of rest for the ark of the covenant, a permanent temple rather than the tent the tabernacle had been housed in originally. His reason was that it pained him to live himself in an extravagant palace while the resting place for the Almighty Holy God was a tent. He wanted the best for Him who is above all. Yet, God's response was a big no. God shared the plans with David and allowed David to do all the preparations of gathering the materials, but David's hands were not to build it. Why? David had too much blood on his hands. In God's words to David, "You are not to build a house for my Name, because you are a warrior and have shed blood" (1 Chronicles 28:3). God did favor David with many special honors in his life, which was peppered with various moments of sin and disobedience, but building the temple, the holy dwelling place, was withheld because his hands were soiled with blood. Instead, God appointed David's son, Solomon, to build the temple, which I am guessing, for David, was the next best thing. He knew that his own eyes would never see it. A bit heartbreaking if you think about it.

Clean hands, living clean—it's of high value in God's economy.

There is yet another parallel to our heavenly Father that I have drawn from the remembrance of my dad's hands in his later years—his deep-red and gold garnet ring. Dad's wedding band was the simplest possible gold band. It drew no attention. But he had this beautiful gold ring with a large garnet stone in it, the setting engraved ornately. It was a gift to him later in his life. After he received this beautiful gift, he wore it almost always. I never really asked him about it, but it was obvious that it was of great value and significance to him.

This ring specifically was what always came to mind when I would read or hear someone speak of a signet ring. A signet ring is one that bares the authority and seal of the king. It carries the identification of being tied to royalty or a specific high-level group or family. It belongs to the one in charge and is worn by one who has the authority to speak and act on behalf of that king, leader, or family headship. It is the kind of ring the extravagant father placed on the hand of the prodigal son upon his return (which I am sure helped incite the intense jealousy noted within the elder brother) from the parable relayed by Jesus in Luke 15.

Like the prodigal son, we are all lost and have a need to return to our heavenly Father through the precious sacrifice of Jesus that bought us forgiveness and a big "welcome" sign with the door wide open to our Father's house. All who receive forgiveness through Jesus Christ and confess His lordship over our lives are received by the Father with that same loving embrace that the lost son experienced. The embrace isn't where it stops, however. We're given that ring. It is symbolic of our inheritance as God's children who bare the honor and authority of our heavenly Father. We may speak and act according to His ways, His will, using His name; and it is sealed by authority that is given to us through the blood of Jesus, as I was reminded by the deep red of Dad's ring. It's not something to be taken lightly because it was bought with the most valuable life that ever walked the earth, God incarnate—God Himself. That blood bought a place amongst royalty as the sovereign King's children, as God's heirs, of which the gold signifies. My dad received that position. His ring reminded me that we all have the opportunity to receive that position and wear that symbolic signet ring as well.

In speaking of Dad's hands with his ring and the blood of Jesus, it comes to mind that the hands of Jesus were of extreme significance as well. Jesus purchased our redemption and bought that place back into God's family with the labor of His own hands. His labor was to stretch those hands forward to heal the sick, raise the dead, cast out demons, lift the shame, feed the hungry, and then stretch them out to be pierced through in sacrifice for us. In doing so, He committed Himself into the Father's hands, as specified in Psalm 31:5 and Luke 23:46.

Remembering the almighty, loving hands of our heavenly Father and the compassionate, victorious hands of the Son is a powerful message that can provide confidence, hope, and strength to our faith. Envision the royal garnet ring sliding off the finger of the Father and being placed as a supernaturally perfect fit onto yours. The royal blood of Jesus was poured out to be shared with you so that a supernatural transfusion could take place. That blood brought you into His bloodline as a royal son or daughter who wears His signet ring of identity and authority. Wow. Think about it. Simple yet profound.

A man's hand with a garnet ring can mean so much. Dad's hands spoke volumes. Receive it all because God gave it not just for me, but all of us who will accept and believe.

10

What Have I Missed?

Life is a journey. I have viewed this journey for most of my adult life as a path riddled with destinations worth pursuing as fast and efficiently as possible. My eyes are fixed on the goals as I run zealously toward each one, always looking just past the one that is closest in front of me, straining toward that which is far beyond in the distance. I have a lot of energy. I am driven. I am happiest when I am busy. I am self-motivated. I don't put things off for later that can be done now because some great fun or adventure might come up later, and I want to be free to embrace it. I am zealous about making the most of every opportunity. I make lists so I don't have to waste time wondering what I should do next or risk forgetting about something that could have been accomplished today.

Are you exhausted yet, listening to how I live my life? I know my husband is! Maybe you are like me with a desire to live every minute to its fullest potential. Maybe you are like my poor husband who gets tired just looking at my lists. When the day is done and I have crossed several things off the list, I have often been plagued with the nagging dilemma of reviewing how I could have accomplished more. In the past, I was often troubled by the frustration of what I *didn't* accomplish rather than enjoying the satisfaction of completing the things that I *did* accomplish. I believe that my perspective regarding my accomplishments has presented one of the greatest challenges of all for my husband throughout the decades of our marriage.

Recently, however, I have begun to understand that life is a journey. The journey is the important part. This has been such a gradual transformation in my perspectives that I can't say it came like the other revelations of my dad. It was more of a slow discovery process. It unfolded as I took time to reflect on daily things around me that began to take on beauty and value, like listening to the sounds of the birds and watching the trees in the breeze or noting the striking beauty of contrast between the vibrant greens of the leaves and brilliant blue of the sky. It came as my husband repeatedly challenged, "Can you enjoy what you did instead of feeling frustrated by what you didn't get done? Feel good about what you accomplished!" It came as I learned to slow down and hit the pause button long enough to drink in the moment and enjoy the essence of what surrounded me.

Looking back on my life, I have realized that I missed a lot of joy. I missed a lot of peace. I ran past a lot of fun. I sped into anxiousness and worry unknowingly by neglecting the enjoyment of the things within my journey. By focusing on maximizing the future, I often missed the beauty of the present. Noticing the divinely inspired traits displayed by my dad that are so clearly an earthly reflection of our heavenly Father's character caused me to ponder the following questions:

- If I wasn't so intensely goal-driven, would I have noticed and enjoyed some of these things about my dad sooner in life?
- Could my vision have been clearer if I wasn't racing through life?
- Would my senses have been keener in perceiving the message conveyed sooner by the touch of my dad's hand that told me he loved having me with him just because he loved me?
- Would my heart have noticed the richness of the inheritance I was receiving years before his death?

- Would I have tasted that hidden sweet honey as a young adult rather than having to wait until it was being poured out at the end of his life?
- What if I had valued the journey as much as I valued reaching the goal?

Learning to enjoy the journey looks something like this for me. On a long road trip through the country, instead of insisting on being the driver or burying my eyes in a book or studying my Spanish so as to not waste those hours, it means fixing my gaze outside, drinking in the uniqueness, the beauty, the people, the homes, the animals of the land. It means observing what's different and enjoying the sites, the colors, the sounds, the changing horizons and skies. It can even be interesting to observe the different license plates and occupants of the vehicles! This is how one time not long ago I discovered some friends of ours who lived in Florida at the time, traveling next to us on the same stretch of highway while passing through Georgia! What a fun surprise! We were both heading to a conference in South Carolina, traveling from different states, and ended up at the same place hundreds of miles prior to our destination. It made for some fun entertainment over several miles as we laughed and communicated through gestures and facial expressions through the windows! I would have missed it completely, though, if I hadn't been enjoying observing the vehicles traveling around us!

We currently live in southern Alabama just a few miles from the Gulf Coast. After having spent my entire life in the north, everything feels different here. I grew up in northern Indiana in Fort Wayne, close to the Michigan boarder. For me, going to college in the southern part of the state at Indiana University in Bloomington, felt like I was really in the south. Following my educational season "in the south," I moved to Minnesota, the true north, where we spent thirty-seven years.

Our relocation to live in Alabama on the Gulf Coast truly feels like a different culture some days—almost as different as being in some of the foreign nations of Central America, South America, and Europe that we have traveled in for ministry work. Only a few of our destinations have felt more foreign to me than this. It literally feels like a different country to me—the landscape and habits of home-owners, the politics, the demeanor of people in public places, even language and accents are barely comprehensible to me sometimes. What northerner knows that a "buggy" is a grocery cart? Or when something takes "a minute," it consumes a longer amount of time than one would expect, possibly even hours, days, or an extreme amount of effort. And I never supposed as a Christian that saying "bless your heart" was an insult to the recipient's intelligence, maturity, or abilities in general. It's like the subject of the comment really *needs* God's blessing because they certainly don't have much else going for them. How many northern folks know that it's definitely not a "sweet" thing to say to someone? There have even been moments when a translator was needed to interpret the strong accent of some pour southern soul trying to communicate with me!

In this most recent journey into the south, however, going to the beach has become a regular destination along the path I am on. In the grand scheme of my life, the beach is like a glorified rest stop on the long road. It can also be considered a regular destination in itself. I have come to enjoy the journey to the beach almost as much as the beach itself. I have taught myself to enjoy the drive anywhere down here as a matter of fact. I love looking for different trees and flowers that I wasn't accustomed to up north. I enjoy taking note of the rose bushes in bloom almost year round. I love seeking out any kind of palm or other tropical plant. The drive is a joy, not just the destination. I have to choose to focus on the beauty, though, rather than the blemishes. There is a good deal of poverty here. There are unkempt yards unlike the manicured lawns and gardens of suburban Minneapolis. There are faded, weather-worn, hurricane-torn business signs. There are piles of discarded household junk awaiting Monday's weekly junk pick up along with refuse from continued hurricane demolition and reconstruction. Massive uprooted tree trunk stubs remain as blemishes reminding me of the worst storm I have ever encountered. I don't dwell on these unsightly interests. I get to choose what my eyes are focused on, so I am forever seeking out that new flower in bloom or the freshly mown lawn. We all get to choose. I can focus on the surroundings by seeking out the beauty or by fixating on the neglected and unsightly. Or I can miss it all completely by being preoccupied with the next thing on my list.

I recall a three-day road trip my husband and I took from Williston, North Dakota, to Foley, Alabama. We decided that, following an intensely stressful previous couple of months, which included the death of one of my sisters from cancer, immediately followed by the birth of our second grandson the very next day, we wanted to take our time and try to enjoy the long drive ahead to return home. This drive proved to me the extent of transformation that has taken place in me as I have yielded myself more and more to allowing God to speak and show me things along the journey. I was noticing the vast differences in the landscape as we went through North Dakota, South Dakota, Nebraska, Missouri, and Arkansas. I found the plains, the hills, the forests, and everything in between all uniquely beautiful. I drank them in like never before, absorbing every small variation. I noticed the different "feeling" in the atmosphere of the places we stopped in different regions. We took time to consult Google and drive down the side streets to explore a beautiful park to stretch our legs rather than the rushed run in and out of the usual roadside rest stop. The journey was important. It was beautifully refreshing. We stopped at a local all-you-can-eat catfish buffet for lunch to enjoy a somewhat shocking, extremely entertaining lunch rather than our customary "grab and eat as you go" fast food while on a long road trip. That catfish meal with its fascinating local clientele, ended up being a highlight on the journey, one we had nearly driven right past and would have missed! The miles in between the destinations have proven to be the richest treasures of all!

Oh, how I wish I had discovered this sooner. I regret that I have more than likely missed many of the joys the Lord had planned purely for my pleasure, but I was in too much of a hurry to notice. In not noticing, I also missed that personal little love note that my heavenly Father had tucked away for me to find.

As a child, I remember many forty-five-minute-long drives to and from my grandparents' lake cottage. Now, a forty-five-minute drive is nothing, but then, it seemed so long! I see that Lord was trying to teach me, even then, to enjoy the journey. I was always either anxious to get to the lake cottage so I could jump in the lake or anxious to get home to finish that Sunday night homework or rest in my own bed. Other times, I would dread the homecoming, not wanting to leave the lake, so I would spend the forty-five minutes lamenting over leaving such beauty and carefree joy behind. Whatever the case would be, I rarely thought about enjoying the country sights. In hindsight, as I discovered in later years, that journey was nothing short of luxurious through corn fields, golden waves of wheat, clusters of cattle, full canopies of towering greenery, and some charming little Midwestern towns sprinkled throughout the route.

My dear dad had tried to teach me the joy of the journey. Often, though not every time, we would stop in the midst of that short forty-five-minute trek for ice cream. He would say things like, "Oh, this darn car! Here it goes again. Where's it going? What's it doing that for? I guess we'll just have to get ice cream again!" My mom made the effort by teaching us road games like counting the cows on your side of the road. When you passed a cemetery on your side, though, you lost all your cows! It became a competition between my sisters and me to accumulate the highest number of cows between towns. Dad would further try to heighten the thrill by pointing out the country hills in advance so we could prepare for our stomachs to get ticked with a speedy coast down the other side. It was all the makings of a mundane, routine journey turned adventurous.

I failed to learn the lesson then, however. It took me another forty-plus years to realize there's joy in the journey, no matter how ordinary. Watching my children with their children, I realize I was far too concerned about getting through to the next stage. I whizzed by some of the enjoyment of the moments that I see now in their children as more than precious. Don't get me wrong, I enjoyed my children, as well as other moments in life, but I also missed a lot. Somehow, I thought by living my life dedicated to Lord Jesus Christ, living for Him, with Him, and in Him, I would have no regrets. Not so. None of us live our lives perfectly. Part of the reason is because we have a sinful nature that causes us to mess up. Part of it, though, is because we lack proper perspective. We lack wisdom. This is something only gained with experience and through our counselor, the Holy Spirit.

Life has a way of training us in what's of value and what is not. It trains us in what is needed to maintain health and strength in the long haul. If we are open to the lessons of life, it teaches us where true joy, peace, and love are found. The more attentive we are to listen, watch, and yield to God's Holy Spirit, the more we grow in this joy, peace, and love. The beauty is that while we don't get to go back and redo those things we missed, God has a way of redeeming the times. It is never too late. It's never too late, while you are still on earth, to begin finding the fulfillment in the journey. I am convinced that life is just as much about the journey as it is the destination. Where you're going is important, but so is what you experience along the way. I am convinced of this because, otherwise, once a person accepts Jesus as their Savior, receives forgiveness, and makes Him the Lord of their life, that person would immediately be taken to be with our heavenly Father. The rest of life on earth would be pointless because we have already attained the goal of an assured destination.

But no, there is much more to be had in this life. The things that you encounter build your character. It also purposefully impacts other lives around you, for the good or bad. My dad had it right with his perspective of expecting purpose for each day he awoke in his last months on earth. Maybe he didn't understand why, but he knew his journey would continue with purpose until the Lord was done, so he would look for it. Dad wanted to be done but he was still present on earth, so he reminded himself that God had something for him to see or do or be that day.

Your story is different than mine. Yet, maybe like me, you feel you've missed some of the joy or peace of experiencing the full love and beauty that surrounds you daily. Be encouraged that whatever you have missed, you can begin to experience now. You can continue on in your journey with new eyes, fresh perspective, and an open heart to see and receive things differently, more fully. One of my favorite prayers from the Bible invites this into our lives. Consider the depth of Paul's words for us as believers from Ephesians 1:17–19a:

> I keep asking that the God of our Lord Jesus Christ, the glorious Father, may give you the Spirit of wisdom and revelation, so that you may know him better. I pray that the eyes of your heart may be enlightened in order that you may know the hope to which he has called you, the riches of his glorious inheritance in his holy people, and his incomparably great power for us who believe.

This is a prayer for wisdom and revelation to know your heavenly Father better. That's what happened to me as I slowed down and began to pay attention to what the Spirit wanted to show me in my surroundings and my family. I began to see the richness in what He had given me already and the beauty of the inheritance I have already in those around me. Life became richer. My anxiousness has decreased while peace and joy have increased with a fresh hope that has grown to become a constant in the way I perceive circumstances, people, and things in my life. I walk daily with an expectation to encounter the heavenly realm in some way. I am frequently reminded that through grace, which I have come to understand as my heavenly Father extending Himself through His Holy Spirit to me, I have HOPE—heavenly opportunities promised every day.

I am not alone, nor have I ever been. Neither have you. Learning to live my life while envisioning His presence with me is as real to me as my dad's physical presence was. It takes the form of picturing Jesus sitting in the car next to me as I drive to work or seeing His hand over mine as I reach out to touch someone. Sometimes it's as simple as tuning in my ears to the impression of His Words as I ask Him in my thoughts, "Father, what do you want to say to this person?" Other times, it can be a picture in my mind of rivers flowing down over me from His throne in heaven or rains washing over me from heaven. I may see a cardinal come and rest close to me in my back yard and sense my Father speaking through it to say, "I am faithful, Peggy, to care for you even more than I care for these precious birds of the air."

These are the kind of encounters we can enjoy when we slow down and keep our ears and eyes tuned into the Holy Spirit who invites us to walk in the kingdom of heaven. The kingdom of heaven is that realm of righteousness, peace, and joy in the Holy Spirit (from Romans 14:17). The righteousness comes from first receiving that free gift of salvation through the Lord Jesus Christ and then being filled with His Holy Spirit regularly, training our ears and eyes to perceive that leading which says, "This is the way, walk in it" (Isaiah 30:21).

When we live our lives with the understanding that the journey itself has as much value as the destination, we are much more likely to hear that direction and see those little signs along the way that add such enrichment to our lives. It's like the thrill of finding hidden treasure in unexpected places. Truly, God is faithful to exceed our daily expectations in life if we are just patient and attentive enough to be looking for Him. He is the prize Himself and He shows Himself in countless, boundless ways. Can you do it? Can you train yourself to stop, look, and listen? You won't be sorry you did!

11

∝

Yield: Proceed with Caution

Is my experience with my dad here on earth unusual or out of the ordinary? I don't think that I am alone in having a father that exemplified many virtuous traits. A lot of people can say they had a "good" dad, meaning, the positives far outweigh the negative traits. Unfortunately, while I would have agreed that my dad was a good man, I had missed some significant godly parallels until late in my life, after my dad was already gone. Had I been more insightful, looking for them, I may have progressed on my faith journey in trusting our Father God a little more rapidly, but then again, I guess I will never really know the answer to that.

Equally, there are many individuals that have the reverse family life experience with a father. Many biological, adoptive or step-dads, display negative traits that far outweigh those of any positive value. Having a deadbeat dad doesn't negate the possibly of learning a lesson or two from him, however. Even if from the perspective of saying, "This is *not* what our heavenly Father is like. This is something that resembles the father of lies," there is still value in looking for the gold in Dad. God specifically instructs us in Exodus 20:20, Deuteronomy 5:16, Matthew 5:19, and Ephesians 6:2 to "*honor your father and mother.*" Though of extreme importance to God indicated by its repetition in both the Old and New Testament, this particular commandment trips a lot of us up because our parents aren't always very honor-worthy. We criticize, blame, judge, make vows that we will *never* be like them, shake our fists in anger and even entertain plots of revenge. Some of that comes from childish, immature perspectives while others have valid reason for responding with such negative reactions. Even "good" parents aren't perfect and, on occasion, do things to elicit sinful responses from their children. Children harbor wounded, angry hearts when there's no explanations, no forgiveness or discipline is administered harshly out of anger without the balance of expressed love.

We are commanded to honor the *position* of our parents, however, as the ones who birthed us, even when their behaviors may not have been very honorable. Honoring a parent that has ungodly behaviors requires us to not focus on the hurtful or sinful qualities every opportunity you get, not talking them down and recounting all they have done wrong repeatedly. It means granting the gift of forgiveness. It means praying for them rather than condemning and blaming them. It requires respect for the natural place of authority they were given, even though they may not have handled their role in a respectful, honorable way. In abusive situations, it can mean walking away or getting help without plotting for painful revenge to make them pay. While God would never ask you to remain in a harmful, abusive situation, we can be removed from the situation and either dishonor with hatred and revenge lodged in our hearts or we can honor with forgiveness and prayer that brings freedom to the heart of the child. I know that (even though I had a good dad) when I recognized some of my own judgments against his actions, forgave him in my heart for his errors and asked our Father in heaven to forgive me for those hidden judgments and vows I had made against my dad, my eyes began to open to a whole new realm of appreciation.

I also saw heavenly parallels that I had missed earlier on. This is one of the ways that the scriptures play out when it says that if you honor your parents, things will go well with you. The inverse implication is that in areas where you dishonor your parents, things will not go well in your life. We reap the negative consequences of making judgments and vows against our parents out of anger, fear, and pain. When we are guilty of dishonor, anger, and bitterness toward one or both parents, we are stuck in that place that results in a veil over our hearts that prevent us from seeing our heavenly Father clearly. We are held back and imprisoned by the very things from our parents that we want to be free from. A lifestyle of forgiveness toward them and asking forgiveness from our heavenly Father for our own sinful responses (even though you may feel justified in them) is the only way to have an open door in your heart to be able to commune with your heavenly Father freely.

We can also make the mistake of transferring traits to our heavenly Father that really aren't like Him at all. We do it subconsciously without thinking about it. We transfer things to God's character that our parents or other significant people in our lives have instilled in us, some with well-meaning, good intentions. It may be something that appears to be a good, noble thing, not necessarily a bad thing. More commonly, many people wrongfully transfer negative traits onto our heavenly Father as well such as God being distant, angry, or watching your every move ready to punish every mistake for example. The negative traits are easier to identify as deception.

What about the seemingly "good" ones? This is where just as much caution needs to be used. By "caution," what I really mean is looking at the scriptures to see if your ideas line up with the Father, Jesus, and Holy Spirit you see described there. The scriptures are where we can find the truth of what His character is really like. Let me give you a couple of examples of things that seemed right but were not biblical at all and consequently led me to misunderstand the heart of our heavenly Father.

I was taught a good work ethic from the time I was small. If you want something, you work for it. That's a good thing. It feels good to work and see the benefit from it. God created us to work actually. In Genesis, Adam was commissioned to watch over the garden and work the land. The curse after Adam's sin of disobedience was the sweat that is associated with difficulty and the thistles or weeds infiltrating and disrupting the fruitfulness of his labor. He would have to deal with hard, painful labor and things that would interfere with a bountiful outcome. In the New Testament (Ephesians 2), it is noted that God has created good works for each of us to do. A good work ethic is good. The problem comes when I equate my value with what

I do or how much I accomplish. This was discussed at some length in the chapter "Holding Hands." Sometimes, a strong work ethic results in a perception of conditional love. In other words, we believe in our hearts that God's love and acceptance is dependent on our performance or what we do or don't do. This is direct conflict with God's unconditional, unfailing love that He has for us. He loved us and saved us while we were still in the midst of our sin. He saved us by grace through faith, not because of any special tasks or work we've done. This is so that no one can boast about what they do or have accomplished to earn that salvation or love. We are only able to love Him because He loved us first. While the scriptures are clear about being able to earn rewards or store up treasures in heaven, it is equally clear that God's love for us doesn't depend on how much we do or earn. It's noble and right to have a good work ethic, but I am not accepted because of it.

Another aspect closely related to that work ethic in my personal story was another unbiblical, ungodly belief that God would only help me if I had somehow earned His help by working as hard as I could and exhausting all other options before coming to Him. It was summed up in this statement that "God helps those who help themselves." This was something that I transferred from my parents to God. It sounds noble. It sounds right. It couldn't be farther from the truth of how God's kingdom operates, however. In the kingdom of God, He helps those who lean on Him, those who look to Him in all things. He causes those who trust in themselves in pride, trusting their own strength to fall.

Please don't misunderstand my point. Leaning on God isn't an excuse for laziness or weakness. It is looking to God *first* for direction, strength, wisdom, or whatever else is needed and then moving out of what we receive, knowing that it has come from Him and not ourselves. We're told to occupy ourselves with faithful good works until Jesus returns, and to be faithful with what He gives us. He expects us to look to Him and His kingdom first and then utilize what He has given us, both in character and physical attributes or resources. He expects us to desire and utilize spiritual gifts. Doing these things results in heavenly rewards that have eternal value. It doesn't, however, earn His love and acceptance. Those were already granted at our conception. Read Psalm 139. There are works, though, that are dead and fruitless. The only work that produces good, eternal fruit is that which comes from Him, as we're connected to Him, not working on our own. John 15 speaks of being attached to Him, the vine, if we're going to bear any good fruit in our lives. Separated from Him, we can do no good thing, nothing of eternal value anyway, which is how He looks at things, with an eternal perspective. There are lots of things we can occupy ourselves with that have no value to Him at all. We can spend our whole lives grinding our wheels, hoping to make it out of the hole, but unless it is led by Him, for His kingdom, these works are described as things that rust, decay, and burn up as stubble in fire. When we come to Him and connect with Him through His Holy Spirit is when help comes. Where does help come from? It comes not from our own muscle and brain power but from Him, the maker of heaven and earth. Out of that connection comes the wisdom and power to help us be and do that which has true eternal value. In fact, Jesus Himself never did or said anything without first getting it from His Father.

Now that I have explained that; I want you to see that my transference of the concept to Father God that I had to do everything I possibly could in a situation before I could ask for His help, wasn't God's nature or way at all! It actually was opposite of His nature. He wanted to be my first go-to and then walk through things with me. He wants to be part of everything I am and do. He's not like Superman that swoops in at the last minute to save us when we we're ready to crash! He's much more like the attentive coach alongside of the student, helping and cheering us on as discussed in chapter 5, "The Coach." Or the careful parent holding the hand of the child to walk us through danger. It doesn't mean that we stand by and do nothing. It's not a lazy gospel. The difference is we do it *with Him*, from the beginning. Because I grew up knowing work and participation was necessary, and I was expected to do all that I could before asking for help, I thought God expected me to work things out on my own, and I could only come to Him with that which was impossible for me. God was a god for the desperate, and while He is that, He's interested in so much more! I have discovered there is so much more joy, peace, and fulfilment walking with Him from the beginning, every day in everything, big and small.

Another aspect of Dad's life that nearly set me in the opposite direction of our heavenly Father's nature was his troubled financial considerations. Dad was always concerned about money, as I mentioned previously. Early on in my relationship with Jesus, I didn't understand the extent of the glorious inheritance I had through Jesus. I often felt the pressure of having to make sure there would be enough—for the kids, my husband, giving to those I felt to bless. It was a battle for many years before I broke through to the revelation of God my Provider.

Working hard and giving our best to produce results of excellence honors God. We always want to do things as doing it for Him, therefore giving Him our best. That is not to be mistaken with being required to work in this way in order to receive anything from Him. I am not independently providing for myself. He is a God of grace, kindness, and patience who loves us always and forever as His children whom He cares for and provides for perfectly. Again, this isn't an excuse for laziness or neglect, but an assurance that we can do what He calls us to without striving and worry. When I felt the Lord calling me to leave my secure corporate job with the nice, regular paycheck to become a stay-at-home mom that in the coming years would mean jumping into piece-meal part-time work as needed to supplement the needs of our growing family, I was able to do so with assurance that provisions come in many ways besides that secure, fat paycheck. Now, with a grown family, I look back and can see that truly, God provided in so many exciting, fun, adventurous ways over the years! With every experience that challenged me to walk each step, listening and leaning on His direction for provision and strength, my faith and love has grown notably. I would have missed so much if I had stuck with the old attitude of God helps those who help themselves. I'm convinced that leaving it all up to me would have severely limited or even thwarted my life experiences and growth.

The point of this book has been to share my path of discovering who my heavenly Father is through having my eyes opened to the spiritual parallels of my experiences on earth. We can't help but transfer some of our experiences in life, especially with our parents, specifically our fathers, to form our ideas of who God is. It is a worthy journey to embark upon to prayerfully consider what your relationship with your dad was like and the dynamics of your family life in comparison to how you view God. It's a journey that must be led by Holy Spirit Himself. But He wants to take you there.

We begin by asking the Holy Spirit to fill you and lead you into truth. Secondly, make yourself a student of the Word of God with regular daily reading, participating in studies that challenge you to dig deeper than just reading at a surface level. Third, yield yourself to become a student of prayer. Ask the Lord to search your heart and show you any ways in you that are misdirected or sinful. He will be faithful to hear your prayers and take you on a journey to make Himself known by you ever increasingly. Don't take for granted that you think you know Him. Never assume you know all there is to know about Him. He is far beyond our full comprehension. Seek Him out in the scriptures, looking for the many places that Jesus reveals Himself as being one with the Father, like Him, speaking what He sees and hears from the Father. Look for confirmation of these things in the Word. In doing so, you will live a life that is full of discovery and fulfillment.

And you will more and more begin to see your Father here on earth as He is in heaven.

12

Everlasting Father

So a funny thing happened the day after I thought I had completed this book. As I was delivering a message over Zoom regarding the love of our heavenly Father, I shared about how God chose the title "father" for Himself. The name wasn't something that one of the great historical prophets or Moses or Abraham chose for Him. God Himself chose it. It matters not how we feel about our own father or fathers in general. God knew that many people would have a difficult time with the terminology, so He sent His Son Jesus, not only as the sacrificial lamb but also to help us get to know our heavenly Father as He really is and close that gap between our perception and truth. Jesus came so that we can know our Father. Just as I spoke in my message the words "Everlasting Father," the term that God chose for Himself from Isaiah 9:6, the Holy Spirit nudged me internally. I continued speaking, but the words kept resonating within me. I hadn't fully considered this title before. I knew the Spirit was speaking what He wanted known. This, which He highlighted that day, is the last bit of insight I will leave you with as we look at our Father revealed to us here on earth.

Our heavenly Father is an *everlasting* Father. I had never really considered what the term implies beyond the fact that our God is eternal. Just a few days before I spoke this message, Jay commented that we're never done parenting our children. The context of that comment was not at all condescending or belittling, but it followed a conversation with one of our adult children. I want you to know that we are extremely proud of our three children. All three have married well, chosen wisely, have their own families, and live in a way that they are an asset to their jobs, in their communities, in their churches. All of them, including their spouses, enrich whatever they are a part of. Though we all live in different states across the country, stretching from the panhandle of Idaho bordering the state of Washington, across to the central US in the northwestern corner of North Dakota cutting into the deep south to the shores of the Gulf of Mexico in Alabama to the eastern most state in the Gulf shores further down in Florida, we maintain a strong connection and love for one another. We literally are strewn from one extreme corner of the nation to the other. Their chosen paths of life are as different as the parts of the country they live in, and believe me, it's as different as a northern winter and summer. Yet all of them periodically look to us for input into their lives. From us, they receive insight, wisdom, perspective, encouragement, and when asked, even direction. Though they don't live with us any longer and have, in fact, "gone into all the world," they still look to us when the need arises. In between those needs, we talk, message, and keep up on one another's lives. It's a high priority for us all to maintain our relationship with one another.

It occurred to me that it was much the same with my parents and Jay's parents. While we lived across the country from one another, in spite of far less technology available, we maintained the type of relationship where we could receive help from them. While we had less frequent yet regular communication, sometimes we would call on them for advice or their perspective. Other times, my parents especially would inspire us to make changes or engage in a new venture or home project. Sometimes they would share a concern or warning. Jay and I never, even when we became parents and grandparents ourselves, stopped looking to them as our parents. Even when they became weak and weary at the end of their lives, we still honored and loved them with the highest respect as our parents, the ones who had gone before us in so many life experiences.

Jay's comment about never being done parenting struck me now as I considered the term "Everlasting Father." Our relationship with our heavenly Father is *ever*lasting. It never stops. *He* never stops. He is always there when we need help. He is always giving us wisdom, insight, proper perspective, encouragement, direction or whatever is needed in the moment. It doesn't matter the length of time we have walked with Him or how we have walked with Him. He is always reachable. He is always approachable. He is always available. How many of us can say the same about ourselves? If we as earthly fathers (and mothers) desire to give good gifts to our children, how much more does our Father in heaven desire to do so? That concept is shown in the scriptures.

> So I say to you: Ask and it will be given to you; seek and you will find; knock and the door will be opened to you. For everyone who asks receives; he who seeks finds; and to him who knocks, the door will be opened. Which of you fathers, if your son asks for a fish, will give him a snake instead? Or if he asks for an egg, will give him a scorpion? If you then, though you are evil, know how to give good gifts to your children, how much more will your Father in heaven give the Holy Spirit to those who ask him! (Luke 11:9–13)

It is repeated in Matthew's gospel.

> Ask and it will be given to you; seek and you will find; knock and the door will be opened to you. For everyone who asks receives; he who seeks finds; and to him who knocks, the door will be opened. Which of you, if his son asks for bread, will give him a stone? Or if he asks for a fish, will give him a snake? If you, then, though you are evil, know how to give good gifts to your children, how much more will your Father

in heaven give good gifts to those who ask him!
(Matthew 7:7–11)

The gift being referenced is the Holy Spirit. Who is the Holy Spirit except the One who gives wisdom, guidance, discernment, and direction? It is the Holy Spirit that reminds us of things we have learned and seen so they can be applied and activated in our lives. This is the Father's gift to us—to be able to receive and walk with His input all the days of our lives! As long as we walk this earth, our Father is still here for us through His Spirit to interact and be involved with us daily as well as during troubled times.

As an adult child to my parents, they never forced themselves on me. I always knew they would give me their perspective if I asked, though. I knew they were there until even at the very end of their lives when they became frail. The point is, I wasn't abandoned or orphaned when I became an adult. Jesus says we must become like little children. Children are ones who still need their fathers. Children depend on their fathers for provision, protection, help, direction, and so many other things.

Ever, always, forever, lasting. He is the Father that doesn't give up. He's like the dad we see watching and waiting for his son to return from running off in rebellion in the story of the lost son from Luke 15. He is the voice that says forgive seven times seventy. He is the One who watches our coming and going and doesn't allow our feet to slip as described in Psalm 121. His is the assurance that He'll never leave or forsake us as noted in both the Old and New Testament (Deuteronomy 31:8 and Hebrews 13:5).

Never forsake us. What does that even mean? We don't really talk like that every day. It means he won't abandon us. Were your parents divorced? Did one of your parents sort of check out, and in their separation, you rarely or never saw them? Or maybe you never saw your dad because he didn't continue a relationship with your mom after you were conceived and was completely absent in your life. Maybe you never met him at all. Or maybe when you turned eighteen, your parents said, "You're on your own, kid," and kicked you out, let you flounder, and suffer in a bad way that had some very hurtful, negative impacts on your life. Maybe you did something like marrying the wrong person or screwing up in some horrible or embarrassing way and your parents disowned you. Father God would never do that. He's in it for life with you—*eternal* life. He's not one to plant a seed in a woman's womb and then walk away and forget that the growing little soul even exists. He watches over all that He creates. All life does begin with Him. You may argue that He can't possibly be involved and love those "seeds" who are seemingly the products of victimization, abuse, or those that have no breath in the world due to abortions or miscarriages. That's for another discussion, although in my life experience with our loving Father, I feel assured that even those not yet fully formed have a place in His heart, and, therefore, a place in His kingdom. He does not abandon the helpless who suffer the effects of a sinful, fallen world where decay and corruption were set in motion as a result of the original sin at the beginning of man's existence. He is a loving Father who always brings hope and life into the dark places of the world. He will never abandon us to leave us in a state of hopelessness. Mankind makes bad choices and uses free will for selfish reasons. It turns its back and walks away to save its own reputation or skin. Abba, our personal "Daddy" God, never does. He never abandons, never leaves, never walks away. In fact, He gave His own skin, His Son, to reunite us with Himself and keep us close.

Forsake means to give up. God will never *give* you up. Maybe you were given up for adoption. Maybe you were given up for the love of money or status. Maybe your parents gave up their time with you for service to a worthy cause or a ministry and it felt the same as being abandoned. Maybe you were given up because your parents couldn't see another way out. Maybe you were even a failed abortion (I personally know some!) in an effort to trade you for personal freedom from the burden of a child. Your heavenly Father wouldn't trade you for anything—nothing because there's no one or no thing that can take your place in His heart. Reread that chapter "Favorite One" if you still struggle with that. He's not going to give you up to another father like the father of lies. He's not going to give you into another kingdom like the one of darkness. You have to choose that for yourself. He won't trade you for anything because He has good plans and a hopeful, prosperous future for you (Jeremiah 29:11). He even created special things just for you to do! (Ephesians 2:10). That means that you have a unique mix of qualities that have custom-made, designer (designed by God Himself) plans awaiting for you to fulfill if you so choose.

God's not going to give up *on you* either. As often as you come to Him in repentance, He will always forgive. What does it mean to come in repentance? Another religious word. It simply means coming to Him ready to and wanting to change. Change your actions, your viewpoint from yours to God's, your perspective from destructive obsessions and desires to ones that lead to life, health, and peace. He never expects perfection, only that you give Him what you have, yourself, as imperfect as that may be. He won't abandon you, deeming you not good enough, because He created you and knows just what you are, with every little hidden wrinkle in your character. In fact, He sent you His perfect Son and covered you with His perfect blood to iron out and cover every imperfection. He paid too much for you to ever give up. You are His irreplaceable, precious masterpiece. He created us with everything we need to live godly, full lives in the time and place that we were born. He knows what we need, and He provided it in advance according to 2 Peter 1:3–4. Everything we need can be found by getting to know Him, by leaning on Him, and by trusting in His great promises to us.

To forsake means to renounce. God won't renounce you. You're His child. When you came to Him to receive salvation by faith in Jesus, by grace (a beautiful gesture reaching down from heaven to answer your cries and intervene in your life), you were marked by His Spirit as His. You belong to Him. He is not ashamed to claim you. He knew you were sinful and fell short before you were even born. Yet He loved you, birthed you, and created a plan for you to prosper. His promise is that He won't renege on His part of the deal, which is to love you and have a relationship with you as His own child if only you will choose Him. He knows how we struggle with faithfulness, yet He promises when we falter and fail in our frail human efforts, He will remain faithful. Always. Forever. Into eternity. Nothing can destroy His faithful love toward us. Not anything. Not ever. It has lasting power through death, life, demons, angels, height, depth, and everything else in all of creation. That's His commitment, His covenant with us. Covenant—another word we use and don't understand. A covenant isn't a bargaining tool or a two-way agreement. God's covenant to us is a one-sided commitment He made to us. He is all in, 100 percent. He won't back down or change His mind because He already paid for that new covenant with His life. It's only dependent on us to the extent of whether or not we accept it. Are we willing to admit we're His? Are we willing to accept the gift of forgiveness? Are we open to let His Spirit come and live, move and have His being in us as a place He's comfortable hanging out in? Is He welcomed in you?

Everlasting Father. The title He chose for Himself. It speaks of eternity. It speaks of that fatherly relationship that will never end, no matter how old, wise, mature, or holy you have become. He's still Father in all His fullness. I am still His girl, His daughter, His Perky Peggy. You're still His son, His child with that special name written on the palm of His hand now and forever. We are forever His.

Amen. So be it!

ABOUT THE AUTHOR

Peg and her husband, Jay, are founders of Passion For Life Ministries Inc., a missions organization equipping and releasing pastors and leaders throughout the US and internationally to share the Father's love, the presence of Jesus, and the empowerment of the Holy Spirit with those who need hope and encouragement. Peg assisted Jay in pastoring a local church for over twenty years and currently ministers together with him internationally. While Peg loves traveling to the nations and loving the ones in front of her, the greatest joy of her life is her family consisting of her husband, their three grown children with their spouses, and grandchildren.

9 798891 123946